D0482566

CALGARY PUBLIC LIBRARY

NOV   - 2010

Advanced Praise for

fixing freddie

"Rounding the hard corners of single parenthood and loss, *Fixing Freddie* is nevertheless an upbeat account of how love and courage are found in unexpected places and lives are changed by the most unlikely heroes."

—Susannah Charleson, author of the *New York Times* bestseller *Scent of the Missing*

"Who let this dog out? Put your paws up and howl for Paula Munier's hysterically funny tale, an incredible journey of the heart. To say the leash, she loves Freddie, and you will too!"

—Julia Spencer-Fleming, Anthony and Agatha Award–winning author of *One Was a Soldier*

"If you love impish beagles, growing boys, a charismatic heroine, and a darn good story, you'll relish every line of *Fixing Freddie*, a breezy memoir that crackles with humor, wit, and infectious optimism. This pet memoir stands heads—and tails—above its competitors, and left me panting for more."

—Susan Reynolds, author of *My Dog Is My Hero*

"Move over, Marley! *Fixing Freddie* delivers laughter, tears, and an abundance of joy."

—T. J. MacGregor, Edgar-winning author of *Out of Sight*

"You don't have to love dogs to love *Fixing Freddie*. It's hilarious, poignant, and totally irresistible!"

—Hallie Ephron, author of *Never Tell a Lie* and *The Bibliophile's Devotional*

"I love this book. It's hilarious. It's heartwarming. It's honest. And it's absolutely charming. One mom's battle with a beagle becomes an inspirational journey for all of us—teaching us about life, loyalty, and the power of love."

—Hank Phillippi Ryan, Agatha-winning author of *Prime Time*

"When a talented comic writer combines a dog, a cat, and a bright preteen boy with attitude, you've got a book full of joyful reading ahead of you."

—Cynthia Riggs, award-winning author of the
Victoria Trumbull series

"In prose as brilliant and fluid as quicksilver, *Fixing Freddie* weaves a rollicking, revelatory story of redemption that all single mothers and single women—make that all women and all mothers—need to read over and over again . . . to remind ourselves that, yes, life is full of mistakes and miseries, but it's also full of triumphs and joys—and it's all fixable."

—Colleen Sell, editor of the bestselling *A Cup of Comfort*
book series, coauthor of *The Everything Kids
Gross Cookbook* and *10-Minute Zen*

"A funny, soulful look at what it means to be a family: *Fixing Freddie* made us sit up, roll over, and beg for more."

—Kathi Kamen Goldmark and Sam Barry, authors
of *Write That Book Already!*

"A heartwarming, refreshing tale of love—human and canine—that will appeal to anyone who loved *Marley and Me*."

—Joseph Finder, *New York Times* bestselling
author of *Vanished* and *Paranoia*

A true story about a boy,

a mom, and a very,

very bad beagle

fixing
freddie

paula munier

Aadamsmedia

Avon, Massachusetts

Copyright © 2010 by Paula Munier
All rights reserved.
This book, or parts thereof, may not be reproduced in any
form without permission from the publisher; exceptions are
made for brief excerpts used in published reviews.

Published by
Adams Media, a division of F+W Media, Inc.
57 Littlefield Street, Avon, MA 02322. U.S.A.
www.adamsmedia.com

ISBN 10: 1-4405-0230-7
ISBN 13: 978-1-4405-0230-9
eISBN 10: 1-4405-0736-8
eISBN 13: 978-1-4405-0736-6

Printed in the United States of America.

10   9   8   7   6   5   4   3   2   1

Library of Congress Cataloging-in-Publication Data
Munier, Paula.
Fixing Freddie / Paula Munier.
p. cm.
ISBN 978-1-4405-0230-9
1. Beagle (Dog breed)—Massachusetts—Humor. 2. Human-animal relationships—
Massachusetts—Humor. 3. Dogs—Behavior—Massachusetts—Anecdotes. I. Title.
SF429.B3M855   2010
636.753'70929—dc22   2010009952

This publication is designed to provide accurate and authoritative information with regard to the subject matter covered. It is sold with the understanding that the publisher is not engaged in rendering legal, accounting, or other professional advice. If legal advice or other expert assistance is required, the services of a competent professional person should be sought.

—From a *Declaration of Principles* jointly adopted by a Committee of the American Bar Association and a Committee of Publishers and Associations

Many of the designations used by manufacturers and sellers to distinguish their product are claimed as trademarks. Where those designations appear in this book and Adams Media was aware of a trademark claim, the designations have been printed with initial capital letters.

This book is available at quantity discounts for bulk purchases.
For information, please call 1-800-289-0963.

Dedication

For my father, who got me my first dog,
and my mother, who let me keep him.

And for Alexis and Corkie, Greg and Rambo,
Mikey and Shakespeare and Freddie—

proof positive that a life without kids and
dogs is really no life at all.

Note to Reader

There are three sides to every love story:
his, hers, and the dog's.

This is her side, and while as true as a howl, the names of various curs, bitches, littermates, pack leaders, and pack followers have been changed to protect both the innocent and the unruly.

"My dogs know more about me than I know about myself."

—ABIGAIL THOMAS, *A Three Dog Life*

Fixer-Upper: *noun,*

something that needs fixing up

chapter one

"Meaning what you say is just as important as saying what you mean."

—JENNIFER BRIDWELL, *The Everything Dog Obedience Book*

WE DIDN'T NEED A DOG. WE HAD A PERFECTLY NICE DOG, A BIG, loveable, huggable, shaggy black mutt from the pound we called Shakespeare. And a cat, a beautiful tabby named Isis. We were a family, me and the dog and the cat and Mikey, my youngest child and the only one left at home. His siblings were grown and gone. His father was just gone.

It was moving day. We'd had many moving days since the divorce a few years before—too many. From Las Vegas to Massachusetts to California and back to Massachusetts once again. And now, from the North Shore of Massachusetts to the South Shore. Only forty-four miles—and a lifetime—away.

"You said no more moving," Mikey had said when I told him about the new job I'd been offered. My dream job, really, as the idea person for a trade house that published some two hundred nonfiction books a year, books that showed readers how to plan their weddings and breastfeed their babies and train their dogs. But that's not why I wanted to take it so badly. The salary was the reason I wanted to take it so badly.

"It means more money, honey." We were sitting outside on the small balcony of our Salem apartment on a cool May evening, watching people walking their dogs and jogging along the crooked and cracked sidewalks below. Our flat took up the middle floor of a tired Victorian-era triple-decker in a neighborhood crowded with tired Victorian-era triple-deckers. "Enough money for a house of our own."

"I like it fine right here." My eleven-year-old son stared out over the rooftops of the city, where a jangle of wires, cables, and antennas met the darkening sky.

"You'll go to a better school," I said. "A safer school."

Mikey looked at me. "My friends are here."

"It's not like we're moving across the country again." I put my arm around his shoulder, but he pulled away. "We'll just be an hour or two away. You can come back and visit your friends any time."

"Right."

"I promise. Any time you want, I'll drive you myself."

"I'm not moving." Mikey folded his arms across his chest, and lifted his pale chin.

I sighed. "We'll talk about it when you come back from your dad's." Mikey was due to leave for California next week, to spend summer vacation with his father as he did every year.

"By then it will be too late." His dark blue eyes filled with tears. "Won't it."

"I'm doing what's best for us, honey."

"Maybe for you." He wiped away his tears with the heel of his hand.

"For both of us."

Mikey stood up, and regarded me with a prepubescent disdain.

"I hate you," he said evenly, and stomped off to his room.

"I know," I said.

While Mikey hid out in his bedroom playing video games, I stayed out on the balcony in the growing darkness. Taking the job meant that after years of financial struggle, I could just barely scrape up the money to buy a house in a decent school district. I never thought I'd be able to do it on my own. And I still wasn't sure that I should, even if I could. Just because I could qualify for a loan, didn't mean I could make thirty years of mortgage payments all by myself. But I owed it to my son to try.

I'd never felt more alone in my life.

I spent the summer looking for houses. The first house I fell for was a remodeled 1800s farmhouse; my offer was trumped by a young couple expecting their first child. The second offer I made on a 1950s ranch home on a lake. It was more expensive, but I thought it was worth it, figuring that even Mikey would like the idea of living on a lake. So I was thrilled when my bid was accepted in mid-June. It was an estate sale; the house was empty and with any luck we'd be in the house by mid-August, just in time for Mikey to start school. But weeks passed without the sellers setting a closing date; finally the family admitted that only four of the five siblings who'd inherited the house were on board. One sibling refused to sign.

I was out of time. I was commuting four hours a day to my new job, and trying to find a house at the same time. Mikey would be coming home soon—but to what? Desperate, I told my realtor to show me every house on every lake on the South Shore. There was only one in my price range—a very small, very expensive, very old fixer-upper with virtually no closets.

I bought it anyway.

And now it was ours. It was just a converted summer cottage really, but the fact that the homely fixer-upper sat on a lovely lake blinded me to all its failings. On this beautiful, crisp, sunny autumn day, lost in the rustle of scarlet leaves and the gentle lapping of the waves and the clean scent of pine, I tried to put my fears behind me and feel happy. I wondered how long it would take Mikey to feel happy here. Three months, six months, a year? The sooner we settled in, the sooner we'd feel at home.

"Time to unpack," I said to Mikey, as we stood on the front deck and watched the moving truck pull out of the driveway.

"Not now," Mikey said. "We have to go get the puppy."

"What puppy?" I considered the prospect of opening the hundreds of boxes crowding the 900 square feet of living space behind us.

"*Our* puppy."

"We don't have a puppy." I wondered how I could squeeze a hundred pairs of shoes into my locker-size closet. Not to mention my clothes.

"But it's time to get one."

"I don't know what you're talking about, sweetie." I didn't do puppies. Mikey knew that. I calculated the cost of putting in a dishwasher once we got settled. No working mom should have to face the dawn without a dishwasher.

"When we get a home of our own, you said," insisted Mikey. "Remember?"

Mikey was twelve now, all legs and arms and attitude. But underneath that bravado was a sad little boy who missed his father—and pulled at my mother's guilt with every reference to our broken family, however oblique.

"I didn't want to move, but I'm here." Mikey turned to face me, placing his hands on my shoulders. "I remembered about the puppy when I was at Dad's house."

"What puppy?" I couldn't believe that Mikey was already nearly as tall as I was. He must have grown three or four inches over the summer.

"We have a home now, Mom, just like you wanted," he said slowly and solemnly, as if he were explaining the nature of the universe to a three-year-old. "It is time to go get the puppy."

Uh-oh. Buried deep in my parental memory I vaguely recalled one of those rationales we serve up when our children want something very badly and we can't—or won't—give it to them. Like cake for breakfast and trips to Disney World and Daddy home for good.

Now, every kid wants a puppy, sooner or later. But puppies were too much trouble—not to mention politically incorrect. Why get a puppy when there were millions of abandoned dogs who needed a home? That's what I always told Mikey, and when that failed to convince him, I always added, "You can't have a puppy in an apartment. Maybe someday when we get our own house . . . ." Over the course of the past twenty years and two marriages I'd loved and lost half a dozen homes to cross-country moves, financial misfortune, and divorce. I became a resigned renter, and abandoned the idea of ever owning a home again. So promising Mikey a puppy on the one-in-a-million chance of home ownership seemed a safe-enough pledge at the time.

Given our paycheck-to-paycheck existence, I never dreamed that the day would come when we would once again live in a home we could call our own. But that unimaginable day was here—the little lakeside cottage was ours. If we lost this home, I would have no husband to blame. It would be all my fault.

"You promised," persisted Mikey.

"But, honey, we have Shakespeare." At the sound of his name, Shakespeare bounded up to us, tail wagging. Shakespeare, the perfect dog, whom I'd adopted and brought home to ease the pain of that first terrible Christmas Mikey and I had spent alone.

Mikey removed his hands from my shoulders, abandoning me for the more loyal Shakespeare. "Shakespeare's great, but he's not a puppy, Mom. When we got him, he was already a *grown-up* dog."

"*And* we have a cat." I searched the yard for our intrepid tabby Isis. "Have you seen her? She must be around here somewhere." Every time we moved I worried that she'd stray too far too soon and never make it back home again. One moving day a couple of years back, a runaway rottweiler chased her into a nearby woods and the terrified feline didn't find her way home for two weeks.

"She's up that tree." Mikey let Shakespeare go, and pointed to a tall maple across the yard. Isis was perched on a low limb, poised to pounce on a squirrel nearly as big as she.

"Puppies can't climb trees," I said, joking. "What use are they, anyway?"

"That's not funny, Mom."

"I know." I paused, and tried another tack. "We just moved in. Maybe once we get settled in—"

"But *you promised.*"

You promised—the two words in the English language most likely to bring a single mother to her knees.

"But," I started, knowing even as I spoke it was another lost cause in a string of lost causes in My Life as Supermom.

"Just like *you promised* we would never move again." Mikey stuck his hands in the pockets of his jeans. He kicked at the loose boards on the porch. I made a mental note to nail them down later.

"We have a house of our own now," said Mikey in a small voice, "so we can get the puppy now."

"We'll see," I said. As soon as the words were out of my mouth I regretted them. In our familial vernacular, "we'll see" was Mommy-Speak for "no way."

Mikey looked up at me with a mild disgust I knew from past experience would soon enough morph into an active adolescent scorn. "So you didn't mean it. You never really meant it."

I looked up at the cloudless blue sky, and sighed. Mikey had left behind his friends, his school, his soccer team—life as he knew it. He was in a new school in a new town, lonely and friendless, as all new kids inevitably were. I was an Army brat, so I knew just *how* lonely.

I thought about the poodle puppy my dad had brought home

to me when I was not much younger than Mikey was now. That little dog—we named him Rogue—had been my one constant friend through a dozen new schools. *God*, how I'd loved that dog.

Mikey wasn't happy about this move, but I was. I had a house, a boyfriend, and a great new job.

I wanted Mikey to be as happy as I was about the move. I sighed again.

We didn't need a puppy. But as all children teach you sooner or later, a promise *is* a promise. And as I was going to learn very shortly, if you don't mean what you say and say what you mean, you've lost the battle before you've even begun.

We started at the local animal shelter. I'd always had good luck—and good karma—adopting animals. Both Shakespeare and Isis were adopted—and if I'd been paying more attention at the time I would have taken their adoption stories as cautionary tales.

Isis came first. Before the divorce, when Mikey was little and we were all living together in California, my ex picked a big fight over one of the three big bones of contention that continually threatened to tear our blended family apart—my job, my kids, my attitude. The next day I received an astonishing floral arrangement of roses and birds of paradise in a big bowl-shaped vase as an apology. Swimming in and around the stems in the water-filled fishbowl was—seriously—a live, lively goldfish. The outré bouquet came with a card—and fish food.

Mikey loved the goldfish, whom he immediately named Freddie. (For reasons still known only to himself, Mikey loves the name Freddie and from the age of three has expressed disappointment that his own name is not Freddie.) Freddie the Fish was our only pet, and the source of much love, attention, and probable overfeeding from Mikey. Within months Freddie succumbed to his watery grave as all goldfish inevitably do.

The fish is dead, long live the fish! I thought as I consoled my heartbroken son, who sobbed and sobbed upon finding his little orange pet floating upside-down in the former flower vase. We buried Freddie the First in a shoebox in the backyard, and I replaced him with Freddie the Second . . . and then Freddie the Third, and Freddie the Fourth. By the time I visited the local pet store in search of Freddie the Fifth, I was totally over fish.

There was a woman there in the store from the ASPCA with kittens for adoption. I didn't know anything about cats, having been raised in a dog lover's household by a now grown farm boy who believed that the only good cat was a mouser in the barn. That and the fact that I was highly allergic to cats had kept me from associating with felines thus far.

There were two kittens left. Sister tabbies, with huge green eyes and the dark striped markings of their tiger cousins. The smaller one regarded me with the cool gaze of an Egyptian queen.

"Aren't they adorable?" The woman from the ASPCA took the baggie that held Freddie the Fifth from my hand and slipped the haughty kitty into my arms.

The kitty purred.

"I don't know anything about cats." I stroked the little princess, whose purrs grew with every caress.

"There's not much to know. Cats can take care of themselves."

"But she's just a kitten." The kitty crawled up my chest and rubbed her soft cheek against mine.

"She's six months old, has had all her shots, and is litter trained." The woman smiled. "She likes you."

"I'm allergic to cats," I said as I nuzzled the kitten.

"I can see that." The woman laughed.

"No, really, I am." I laughed, too.

"People who are allergic to cats are often allergic to the saliva that's deposited on the fur when they clean themselves," she told me.

"There's a spray you can use to wipe the cat down before you pet it, which neutralizes the allergens."

"Yeah, I've heard of that. There's a guy at work who swears by it." My friend Brett was always encouraging me to adopt a kitten for Mikey, and swore by this spray.

"And even if you are allergic, it won't be near as bad with a female cat. Female cats secrete less of the allergen . . . ." The cat lady trailed off, letting the fearless feline do the sales job for her.

The little kitty had curled up in my arms and was now dozing off. I waited for the sneeze that never came. "Well," I told the woman with a grin of surrender, "I guess I'm just allergic to *other people's* cats."

Fifty dollars and an adoption kit later, I was in the car and on the road with a mewing cat in a box and an unsuspecting fish in a bag. By the time I pulled into the driveway, I'd named the regal kitten Isis after the Egyptian goddess. Four-year-old Mikey loved her at first purr, even when only hours later she slapped a lightning paw into the fishbowl vase and slurped down Freddie the Fifth—a portent of victims to come. She's been the favored animal in the house ever since.

Shakespeare was another impulse I couldn't resist. We were in Las Vegas by then. We moved there when Mikey was five to make a new start—but within six months my husband and I were living in separate apartments. (Note to self: Never move to Vegas to save your marriage.) There was no book publishing in Nevada, so I'd returned to the newspaper business. Vegas was such a transient city—thousands of people moving in and out every month upon the rise and fall of their fortunes—that abandoned animals were a huge problem. There were too many animals—and too few adopters.

The newspaper where I worked sponsored an adoption day at the pound every year. It was a Saturday event in early December, the hope being people would be moved to take home a pet as a present for Christmas. I was obligated to stop by as a show of support. Mikey was with his dad for the weekend, and I was shopping with my mom.

"We have to drop by the park," I told her. "Just for a minute, you know, put in an appearance."

"Uh-huh." Mom knew what a sap I was for a fundraiser. I bought light bulbs from the disabled, magazines from disadvantaged youth, tickets to square dances from local law enforcement.

When we got to the park and Mom heard the barrage of barks, she raised an Elizabeth Taylor eyebrow at me. When she saw the "Adopt a Dog Today" sign, she pursed her perfectly lipsticked lips at me, shook her chicly cut mane of shiny white-as-snow hair, and clucked. "You don't need a dog."

"Mom, I'm not here to adopt a dog. I'm here to support the event."

"Uh-huh."

We looked around the greenspace. There were volunteers walking dogs of every breed, shape, and size up and down the paths throughout the park, in an effort to drum up business. I tried not to look.

"Let's go see if there's anything we can do to help." I pointed to the tent across the park.

We made it about halfway there when we were spotted by a painfully thin, scraggly mutt that once upon a better time might have been a briard or Portuguese water dog. The poor pooch trotted up to us, his elegant gait a hint of his former glory. A desperate volunteer followed close behind, leash in hand.

The shabby dog looked at me with dark brown eyes nearly hidden under a shock of scruffy bangs. He dipped his head and pushed his nose under my hand for a little affection.

"Oh, poor baby!" I squatted down and hugged the sweet dog. "Why is he so thin?"

"You should have seen him when we found him. On the verge of starvation, hiding in a shed at the back of a foreclosed property."

"Oh no!" I gave him another hug. "Who did that to you?"

"Why isn't he on a leash?" My mother glared at the volunteer.

The volunteer ignored her, the obvious dog hater. She turned her attention to me, the obvious dog lover. "He's such a good dog. I couldn't bear to keep him on the leash."

"He *is* a good dog." I scratched him behind his long, loopy, ears. "You are *such* a good dog. Mom, is he cute or what?"

"Uh-huh."

"What's his name?"

"Well, we call him Blackie, but we really don't know. He came to us as a stray."

"A stray," my mother repeated. "God knows where he's been."

"He has such a dignity about him," I said. "If he were mine, I'd give him a grand name, like . . . Shakespeare."

"You don't need a dog." My mother's cultured voice was firm.

I straightened up. "No, of course not. We're just here to help out."

The volunteer sighed. "It's his last day. He's been with us three months. If no one adopts him today, we have to put him down tomorrow."

"Oh my God." I looked at my mother.

"Don't even think about it."

"You can have him for free." The volunteer persisted. "We'll waive the adoption fee."

My mother sighed. "You do not need a dog."

"Christmas is coming, Mom." By this time my ex and I had separated and reconciled more times than I could count—with the reconciliations typically happening at Christmas. "Mikey and I will be all alone."

"You have the cat."

"You know how I get at Christmas."

"You cave. You cave every time." My mother did not like my ex, and did not want me to cave again this holiday season.

"Not this time, Mom." I tousled the dog's topknot. "Remember in that movie *Wall Street* when Michael Douglas says to Charlie Sheen, 'Need a friend? Get a dog.'?"

My mother nodded.

"Well, 'Need a husband?'" I paused.

"Get a dog." My mother took the leash from the volunteer's hand. "We'll take him."

I insisted on paying the fee—it was my own company's fundraiser, after all—and we put the delighted dog in the back seat for the ride home. He settled right down, calm but alert and ready for adventure.

"He *is* well-mannered," my mother said, undoubtedly comparing him favorably with my ex. "And he'll make a good running companion for you." My mother worried every time I set out alone on one of my morning jogs through one of Las Vegas's treeless parks.

"Yes." I smiled, thinking of how thrilled Mikey would be—and how fun it would be to watch him tell my ex that I'd gotten our son a dog.

Isis and Shakespeare had proven more than worthy companions during the ups and downs of the next several years. With the all-knowing Isis settling on our laps whenever we were blue and the loyal Shakespeare guarding our front door by day and our beds by night, they were a comfort and a joy to both me and Mikey during good times and bad.

But now Isis was nine years old and Shakespeare was seven years old, at least as far as we knew. So maybe Mikey was right, and it was time for a new addition to our little family, now that we had the cottage. We set off for the local pound with high hopes.

But there were no puppies at the pound on the South Shore. The responsible citizens of the Commonwealth of Massachusetts were apparently so politically correct that they neutered their animals just as they should without fail, drastically cutting down on the number of available puppies. There were plenty of older dogs and a plethora of older cats, but no puppies.

"We do get puppies in from time to time," Shelley the volunteer told us. "But why wait, when there are so many nice dogs here you can choose from. Great dogs who need a good home—and would love to live with you." She gave Mikey a significant look.

"We're getting a *puppy*. Today." Mikey stared Shelley down, then turned on his heel and walked out.

I sighed. "I'm sorry," I said to Shelley. And raced out the door after my stubborn son.

I'd spent a lifetime running after wayward males. What was one more?

chapter two

"The most serious problems in owning a dog arise because the initial selection was made thoughtlessly or in haste."

—ROGER A. CARAS, *Harper's Illustrated Handbook of Dogs*

THIRTY MINUTES LATER WE WERE BACK AT THE COTTAGE AND MIKEY was on the laptop searching for puppies on the South Shore.

"Find anything?" I sat down next to Mikey on the couch with a bag of Doritos, the only food in the house. The new refrigerator wasn't being delivered until Monday, so I'd yet to stock up on groceries.

"Nothing down here." Mikey cast me a baleful look, then thrust his fist into the bag. "The South Shore sucks," he said through a mouthful of chips. "That's what all my friends back home in Salem said and they were right."

Back home.

"Don't talk with your mouth full." I held the bag of Doritos out away from him. Mikey lunged for them. "This is home now, our own home, the one we always wanted, remember?"

"The one *you* always wanted," Mikey said.

We wrestled for control of the chips.

In the tussle the bag tipped, and we were showered with Doritos. We scrambled for ammo and pelted each other with chips.

"The South Shore sucks!" Mikey tossed a handful at me.

"The South Shore rocks!" I yelled, laughing, as I returned fire. Shakespeare trotted over and helped himself to the leftovers.

Mikey went back to the computer. I gave Shakespeare a hug.

"Look all you want, we already *have* the best dog in New England. You'll never find another one this good."

"There's a place called the Puppy Palace in Bowlington."

"Bowlington? That's hours away."

"No, it's not." Mikey pounded the keys. "Forty-eight miles. Right off the turnpike."

He smiled at me, triumphant. "They're open until five. If we leave now, we'll make it in plenty of time." Mikey jumped up and ran into the kitchen. Back in a flash with my purse in one hand and my keys in another, he presented the purse to me with a flourish, then held up the keys and rattled them. "Come on, Mom, let's go!"

It thrilled my mother's heart to see my boy so excited about something new. He'd had a lot of new lately—new house, new neighborhood, new school—that he was *not* so excited about. How could I deny him this one small thing?

I watched him as he tore out of the room and then out of the house, Shakespeare on his heels. The door slammed behind Mikey, stopping Shakespeare short. He sat there, tail wagging, whining to be let out.

"Sorry, Shakespeare." I patted him on the head, and pointed to his bed. Shakespeare gave me a mournful look, and then shuffled off to sleep away the hours until our return.

Mikey was already in the car.

"This is no way to get a dog," I complained as I started the car and pulled onto the rutted dirt road that passed for our street. "We have no idea what this place in Bowlington is like. It might be one of those horrible puppy factories PETA is always going on about."

"What's PETA?"

"People for the Ethical Treatment of Animals," I told him. "It's an organization dedicated to making sure that animals are treated well by us humans." We bounced along for nearly half a mile in silence until we reached the point where our so-called road hit Route 14.

"We're animals, too," Mikey said, finally.

"True." I stole a glance at my son. "But we aren't always nice to the other animals in our jungle. Like with these puppy mills, where they breed puppies in crowded, unsafe conditions just to make a quick buck." I turned onto the county road and headed for the freeway. We passed through the little village center, past the common with its Victorian-style bandstand and the white clapboard town hall, police station, and historical society. The big old trees shimmered in gold and red and yellow. New England at her finest. After twenty years out in La La Land, the timeless rhythm of this Yankee country's seasons provided me with a profound sense of security. We were safe here.

"They hurt the puppies?"

"Sometimes. But mostly they just treat them badly, so that they're sick and overbred and lots of trouble when they grow up." *Just like kids*, I thought to myself.

Mikey looked at me. "Trouble how?"

"Some dogs turn out too timid, or too anxious. And some just turn out too mean." *Just like husbands*, I thought again. We zipped up the ramp to Route 3, and were on our way to Bowlington.

"Can't you train them?"

God, I hope so, I thought. "Some dogs are untrainable."

"I bet Papa Colonel could train them," Mikey said, with a boy's unshakeable belief in his grandfather. Although in truth we all felt that way about my dad. The Colonel was the man you called when you needed someone to rescue POWs or negotiate with hostage-takers or chew out teenage miscreants. Or train your dog. He'd raised Weimaraners and German shorthaired pointers and Great Danes—there wasn't a dog alive he couldn't master.

When I was eight he was stationed in Korea for a year; Mom and I stayed back home in Fort Sill with Dad's latest dog, a lively young and strong vizsla named Red. Red was perfectly well behaved until the Colonel set foot on that plane for Asia. From then on Red was completely unruly; he lunged at postal workers, assaulted male visitors, and barked at everyone else. Mom—not a dog person—was scared of him. I loved him but was far too young to tame the eighty-pound beast. The day he cornered our family priest Father George in the dining room was the day Mom took him to a kennel to stay until Dad came home.

Six months later the Colonel returned from Korea, and after greeting Mom and me warmly, his first course of action was to go get Red. We drove out to the kennel through miles of nothing but tumbleweeds and tarantulas in Dad's new Buick, he at the wheel, Mom in the passenger seat, and me in the back seat. Just like life was supposed to be in 1965.

Some twenty minutes later, we pulled up to a rambling compound cheerfully marked "Kennel," and we all piled out of the car. Dad strode to the entrance, Mom and I trailing behind.

"I'm here to get Red, the vizsla," he told the lanky guy with the buzz cut and the Okie twang. The name on his shirt pocket read Bob. Bob ran the place.

"That dog's crazy," Bob drawled.

"I told you," Mom whispered to Dad.

"Nonsense."

"Should be put down." The guy looked at my father, took in his perfectly pressed uniform and the gleaming silver oak leaves on his shoulders. "Sir."

"Nonsense," Dad repeated. "Let's see him."

We followed Bob and Dad through the kennel, a noisy, strong-smelling warren of fenced pens full of noisy, strong-smelling dogs. We passed German shepherds and golden retrievers and Irish setters, black Labradors and Weimaraners and bloodhounds, beagles and bassets and dachshunds. All lively, loud, tail-thumping dogs hoping that we were coming for them. But we weren't. We kept on walking, past dozens and dozens of cages. Finally, at the very back of the kennel, in a pen taller than the others, a crazed streak of growling, snapping aggression flung itself against the wire walls over and over again. Red.

"Wow." I turned to my mom. "What happened to him?"

"I told you that dog was out of control," my mother said to my father. He ignored her. My mother held me back as Dad approached Red.

"Let me get the hook for him," Bob said.

"Unnecessary." My father reached for the latch on the cage.

"I wouldn't go in there if I were you," Bob was yelling now, so he could be heard over Red's wild barking.

The Colonel opened the door. Red leapt.

"Down, Red, down!" commanded the Colonel in the voice I knew from personal experience could bring little girls and grown men alike to tears.

Only Bob was surprised when Red stopped mid-lunge and dropped to the cement floor with a whimper.

"Come!" Dad put his hand out and Red crawled to him, tail wagging at warp speed. Dad patted Red's head and scratched his ears. "Good dog."

The Colonel walked out of the cage, Red at his heels. "We'll see ourselves out," he said to Bob.

Bob grinned. "Yes, sir."

Dad would approve of my getting Mikey a puppy. After all, he helped my daughter Alexis adopt a cute little Welsh corgi from the pound for her tenth birthday; when my son Greg turned eleven he and the Colonel came home with a rottweiler–Great Dane mix. He believed that dogs were good for kids—and vice versa.

"You're right," I told Mikey. "Papa Colonel can train any dog." *If only he were here in Massachusetts instead of thousands of miles away in Las Vegas—then he could help us train this new puppy,* I thought. "But we're on our own," I told Mikey. "We'll have to train this puppy ourselves."

"Piece of cake," Mikey said.

Piece of cake.

The Puppy Palace sat just inside the city limits of Bowlington in a large old Victorian home. Clean and cheerful, it looked more like a well-run daycare center than the sordid puppy mill of my imagination.

"We're here for a puppy," Mikey told the sweet-faced, white-haired dog breeder at the front desk.

"Are you now," she said, her voice full of Irish smiles. "Well, you've come to the right place, young man." She pointed to the left. "Why don't you take a look at the wee ones, then?"

Mikey bounded down the hall toward the irresistible call of joyful puppy noise.

"Thank you," I said to the puppy lady, and hurried after my son.

I found him in a big, bright room that had once been a sun porch. Playpens full of adorable puppies lined the walls. Tiny and fluffy and yappy little pooches, too lovely for words—a stylish cacophony of eight-week-old Yorkies and Shih Tzus and Lhasa apsos. Toy poodles and Chihuahuas and Pekingese. All of whom would fit perfectly into a Kate Spade bag, even once they were full-grown. *If Paris Hilton were running a kennel*, I thought, *this would be it.*

Mikey ran from one puppy to another, excited and happy. "Look at this one, Mom! Look at this one!"

They were all beyond cute, but I knew that these pretty puffy balls of beribboned fur were far too feminine for my boy. Oh, at twelve he might fall head over heels in love with one; but by fourteen he'd die of testosterone-driven embarrassment before he'd be seen walking such a girly dog in public. He certainly wasn't going to carry it around in his purse. If we went home with one of these trendy creatures, the chi chi canine would end up being mine—not Mikey's. And I already had a perfectly good dog in Shakespeare.

"They are darling," I said, noncommittal. I moved from playpen to playpen, desperately seeking a manly little dog. One who wouldn't look so good in a pink puppy tutu.

It had been a long time since I'd actually *purchased* a dog. Our pets had always come from the pound, ours for only a small donation and the cost of spaying when required. But these designer pups were purebred beauties—with price tags to match. The average price of a puppy here was $500; some brought as much as $1,000. I calculated the state of my meager savings, recently depleted by the extra closing costs on the house that had run me $4,000 I had not expected. I still needed a washer and a dryer, curtains and rods, a dishwasher . . . and all the other sundries you needed when you moved into a new home. Not to mention as a proud homeowner I'd just doubled my monthly expenses in mortgages, taxes, and property insurance. The raise that came with my new job helped, but for the first time in forever I'd actually need the child support that by law I should receive but in fact rarely did. I'd informed my ex that he needed to start paying support more regularly now, but that was no guarantee I'd actually get it, short of hiring a pricey attorney in California to make it happen. More money I didn't have. I shut my eyes, and wondered—not for the first time—how I could possibly pull off the perfect suburban family life as a single mom.

"Mom?"

I opened my eyes to find Mikey standing before me, holding a wriggling white powder puff with two dark eyes and a pink tongue that licked Mikey's cheek with vigor.

"Isn't she cute?"

"Yes," I said slowly, looking out of the corner of my eye at the price tag on the bichon frisé's pen. $1,000. There went my washer and dryer. I turned my attention back to my son. "She's adorable *now*. But she won't be a puppy forever. She'll grow up into one of those frilly lap dogs. Are you really going to want a *girly* dog to call your own when you're fourteen . . . sixteen . . . eighteen?" I held my breath.

Mikey thought about that, then handed me the puppy. "You may be right, Mom. We'll just have to get a bigger dog. A guy's dog, like a black Lab or a golden retriever." He looked around. "I don't see any of those here. This is a small-dog place."

"Whoa, buddy." I set the little bichon frisé carefully back down in her pen. "We already have a big dog. And a cat. And you and me in the world's smallest house."

"But, Mom . . . ."

"We agreed that you'd get a small dog. There has to be something here." I pushed Mikey toward the back of the room. "Let's keep looking."

I spotted a pair of dachshunds. "Now those are cute. But not *too* cute."

"I don't want a *wiener* dog, Mom."

"Okay, okay." I laughed. "How about this little pug? Pugs are great dogs."

Mikey leaned toward me. "I think they're kind of ugly," he whispered, so as not to offend the jowly little puppy.

"I see." We were nearly to the end of the line of pens—and running out of options. If I didn't find the right pup fast right here at the Puppy Palace, I'd soon be tripping over some drooling, lumbering, 200-pound Saint Bernard in my postage-stamp living room. *Please God*, I thought.

And then I spotted him. The answer to my puppy prayers. A sweet, silky-eared beagle baby, sleeping peacefully in the midst of all the yipping and yapping of his fussy little puppy peers.

"Look," I said to Mikey, "it's Snoopy!"

"Shush, Mom, he's sleeping." Mikey leaned over the pen to get a closer look. At the sound of my son's gentle voice, the little beagle opened his big brown eyes and looked right into Mikey's heart. He was a goner.

"See? You woke him up."

"That's okay," I said, smiling at Mikey's newly paternal tone. "Why don't you introduce yourself?"

Mikey reached in and pulled the drowsy dog up into his arms. "He's so soft. Feel his ears, Mom."

I scratched the puppy's sleek, russet-colored ears. He *was* cute. And he seemed so mellow. Mellow was good. We needed a puppy who wouldn't annoy his elders, namely Shakespeare and Isis. The affable Shakespeare might overlook some youthful antics, but the exacting Isis undoubtedly would not. That wise feline did not suffer any fools—read dogs—gladly. A harebrained hound could find himself on the wrong side of the cat's claws in a flash.

"Why don't you take him to our playroom?" The white-haired puppy lady appeared as if on cue to seal the doggie deal.

Mikey grinned. "Cool."

"It's the door just past the last pen."

I watched my son cradle the little dog in his arms like the big baby he was and carry him carefully into the playroom.

"He's larger than these other puppies," I said, considering the relative size of the little balls of fluff yapping around us.

"He's a bigger breed. And he's older."

"Older?" I raised an eyebrow.

"He's six months old. Most of these puppies are six to eight weeks old."

I frowned. "Does that mean there's something wrong with him?" Surreptitiously I checked out the price tag on his pen: $500. I was *not* spending five hundred bucks on a defective dog.

"It means he's had all his shots and is housebroken." She smiled at me.

"Housebroken," I repeated. *What a beautiful word.*

"Let's see how they're doing together, shall we?" She led me into the playroom, where Mikey was on his hands and knees, giggling as his new best friend licked his face all over.

"Yuck," I said. "Doggie cooties."

"Oh, Mom." Mikey rolled his eyes. The dog kept on licking.

"I guess he likes you."

"Yeah." Mikey laughed. "I like him, too. He's the one, Mom."

"Are you sure? We don't know anything about beagles."

"We don't need to know anything. He's a good dog."

"We could go home, research beagles online, and then come back . . . ." My voice trailed off.

"Mom!"

"We send puppies back to the breeder if we haven't sold them by the time they're six months old," said the puppy lady. "He's due to go back Monday."

"We'll take him," Mikey told her. Then he fixed me with his sternest gaze. "We're taking him, Mom."

"How much is he?" I asked her, knowing full well I was about to shell out my dishwasher money for this loveable lump of fur.

"Usually five hundred," she said, "but since it's his last weekend, he's actually on sale."

I loved a good sale. "So?"

"Fifty percent off."

Only $250. Such a deal. Visions of dishwashers danced in my head. "Sold!"

The puppy lady smiled.

Mikey whooped.

The startled puppy yelped.

And so the howling began.

chapter three

"[Dogs] lie beside us in the darkness, companions of the
night, eager to greet us at the coming of dawn."

—THERESA MANCUSO, *Who Moved My Bone?*

"WE'LL CALL HIM FREDDIE." MIKEY SAT IN THE BACK SEAT WITH the puppy on his lap while I drove us home to Lytton.

"Of course we will."

I had his papers—yes, Freddie the Purebred came with Universal Kennel Club International documents that declared his blood lines perfect—and his shot records, his puppy food, treats, and leash in the Puppy Palace bag on the front seat. I stole a look at Mikey, who was stroking the little dog from his head to tail. Freddie had curled up into a tight ball, his nose tucked into the space between Mikey's knees. He was snoring lightly, a whimper that whispered throughout the car. It was a sweet sound common to all babies, one that after three babies of my own nearly always brought me to tears. Now Mikey had fallen under its spell—and Freddie would be the luckier for it.

Halfway home, Mikey fell asleep, too. I drove on toward our little cottage, content in the happy silence of my boy and his dog.

I was happy, too. More important, I was proud.

Proud that I was doing right by Mikey. I loved my kids, but my love wasn't enough to give them a stable life. For a smart woman, I'd made more than my fair share of stupid mistakes—most of them husbands. My first husband left me broke with two small children, no college degree, no work experience, and no job prospects. My second husband left me broke with one small child, two teenagers, a roofless house, one cat, and a small fortune in unpaid taxes. Not to mention a custody battle that cost me my life savings and several months of my life. I'd survived those disasters, and my kids had survived them, too. But you're supposed to do more than help your kids survive, you're supposed to help them thrive.

For the first time since we moved, I believed that I had done the right thing, after all. We had a house, a future, a life, where we had had none before.

These unexpected gains in the face of the losses we had suffered in recent years were nothing if not miraculous.

If only we could hold on to them.

We dragged the big crate that had borne Shakespeare from the West Coast to the East Coast in the hold of a jet plane in from the garage and set it up at the foot of Mikey's bed. I folded up one of Mikey's old bedspreads—Superman to the rescue!—and placed it in the bottom of the crate.

"This smells like you," I told Mikey, "so Freddie will like it."

"Why can't he sleep with me?" Mikey held the sleeping puppy in his arms while I prepared his new sleeping quarters.

"No dogs on the furniture," I said sternly. "Shakespeare sleeps on the floor. Freddie sleeps on the floor."

"Mom," whined Mikey.

I held firm, pursing my lips to show that I was dead serious about this.

When whining didn't work, Mikey tried reasoning with me. "Isis sleeps with you."

"Isis sleeps *on* me," I corrected him. "But she's a cat. Cats sleep wherever they want. There's no stopping them. Dogs are different. Dogs are trainable."

"He's just a baby, Mom."

Mikey pronounced "baby" with the same sweet sentimentality I always gave the word, and for a moment I thought the little upstart might be mocking me.

"You always let me sleep with you when I was a baby," Mikey added.

Ah, no, he wasn't mocking me, he was simply pandering to my maternal instincts. And naturally it worked. The truth was, I let all of my children sleep with me far longer than the experts advised. When they were little, my older children Alexis and Greg each had their own rooms, and went down for the night in their own beds, but by dawn they were always happily nestled against one side of me or another, having crawled into my bed sometime after midnight. Husband #1 was rarely home, so he didn't mind.

It was only after the divorce, when we were forced to vacate the family home and take up residence in a small flat where they shared a bunk bed in a room not much bigger than a walk-in closet, that Alexis and Greg stopped sneaking into my bed every night. They didn't need me to protect them from the dark anymore; they had each other right there, only a dream away.

Things were different with Husband #2, who was always home. Mikey slept with his father and me from the day we brought him home from the hospital. We couldn't bear to leave him in his little crib, this miracle baby we never thought we'd have. We had both been married before, and had children from our first marriages. We thought we were through having babies, but after we wed, we realized that we wanted a child to celebrate our union, and to cement our blended family. So my ex braved a vasectomy reversal at forty, and I braved a third pregnancy late in my third decade. Mikey was the blessed result of this unexpected audacity—and despite our many differences, we were one in our affection and love for this adorable child we'd brought into the world together against all odds.

Mikey had his own bedroom early on—but he rarely slept in it. By the time he was in kindergarten his older siblings were grown and gone, our marriage was faltering, and Mikey became the cuddling glue that kept us together in the same bed, the same house, the same life. But the glue didn't stick.

We fought and broke up and made up over and over again. We loved each other, and we hated each other. We loved our little family, and we hated our little family torn asunder. So we endured a series of angry partings followed by short-lived reconciliations, followed again by angry partings.

This went on for years. Desperate to end the cycle of mending and tearing and mending, I finally took a job on the East Coast and escaped with Mikey to Massachusetts. We couldn't live apart so close together—so I got a quickie Vegas divorce and put thousands of miles between us. When I left my ex so far behind, I hoped that this would be the break that stayed broken.

Mikey was used to sleeping by himself in his own room by that time, but every night before he went to sleep he would bring me a photo of his father and me in happier days.

"Say goodnight to Daddy, Mommy," he would instruct, and driven by equal parts guilt and love I would do as I was told.

After we left, Mikey's father waged an unrelenting campaign to get us back—and within less than a year I caved. Disney called and offered me a great job in California, where my ex had returned to live after Mikey and I moved east. I took that as a sign that we should join him there. I said goodbye to Joel, the lovely man I'd been dating, saying that the Disney opportunity was simply too lucrative for me as a single mom to decline. To Joel and the world—not to mention my mother—I was only answering the siren call of Tinkerbell. To Mikey and his dad, I was going home so we could be a family again.

Joel insisted on driving us to the airport, and as guilty as I felt I didn't know how to get out of it. He was a big, laconic guy with the kind of rugged face that could have made him a B-list movie star in old 1950s Westerns, if he'd been so inclined. But under those tough-guy looks lurked a surprisingly gentle spirit, which took me by surprise at the most awkward moments. Like now.

"He's crying, Mom," Mikey said, head turned back at Joel as I pulled him toward the gate.

"Don't look back," I told Mikey, wiping away tears of my own. "Don't look back." No man had ever wept over me before—and for one brief shining moment I worried that I might be making a mistake. Then I shook my head to clear away any thoughts of the man I was leaving behind, and plowed into the future, my son in tow.

It was St. Patrick's Day—a lucky day to be returning to my handsome Irish ex. Or so I thought. But our luck changed early on. Snow fell heavily in Boston; we waited in our seats on the plane several hours on the ground at Logan Airport while they de-iced the wings of the plane again and again. By the time we arrived in California, it was nearly ten at night. Mikey and I were tired and hungry but thrilled and excited, too.

I suspected I'd made a terrible mistake the minute I spotted my ex at the airport. He wore that hooded look I'd come to recognize as a danger sign. Mikey ran ahead, and his dad hugged him tight.

"You look great," he said to me, without really looking at me. Something he always said when he had something to hide. My ex gave me a quick kiss, avoiding my eyes, and then hurried us through baggage claim and out to the car.

The San Tadeo night sky was gray, the air damp. It started to rain. My ex didn't say much, just kept his eyes on the road.

"I'm hungry," Mikey said.

"I'm sure you are." I turned to his father. "We haven't eaten for hours. Can we stop somewhere on the way home?"

"Don't have time."

I looked at him, but he wouldn't look back.

I was confused. He'd begged us to come back to him, and now that we were here, he was behaving as if he didn't really want to see us, as if he didn't really want us here at all.

"How about Jack in the Box, Dad? That won't take long." Mikey jumped up and down in his seat. "They don't have Jack in the Box in Boston."

But his dad didn't take us to Jack in the Box. He didn't take us home. He simply dropped us off at the condo Disney had provided for us until we could find a place of our own.

"I'll be back Monday to take Mikey to dinner," he told me, and turned to leave.

"What?" I watched him walk away. "Where are you going?"

"Daddy!" Mikey ran after him.

I stood there, unable to move, to speak, to breathe.

"Go back to your mother."

"What are you doing?" I asked again.

"Nothing," my ex said.

"Why are you leaving?" My voice rose. "Why are you leaving?"

"You divorced me and moved to Boston," he said.

"But we came back."

"You divorced me and moved to Boston," he repeated, the muscles in his jaw tightening as he spoke.

With those words, I realized that it had all been a scam, payback for divorcing him and moving to Massachusetts. We'd just moved 3,000 miles to be a family again, but he didn't want us to be a family again. He didn't want us. At least he didn't want me.

Mikey started to cry.

I didn't know what to do. Mikey would never understand why his father was leaving without him when we'd just gotten here. It would break his heart. My old heart had been broken many times already; one more time wouldn't kill me. But Mikey's heart was young and unscored; he adored his father and was not prepared for this sudden wallop.

I stumbled toward them, swallowing my own grief and rage just long enough to save my son's hurt feelings. "Take Mikey with you. You can have him for the weekend."

"No room at the studio. Besides, I have other plans," my ex said, dismissing us both. "I'll pick him up on Monday."

He had never refused to take Mikey before. Ever. In fact, he usually pushed for every possible moment with his son.

I stared at him. "How could you do this?"

"You divorced me and moved to Boston," he said for the third and final time. And then he strode to his truck, threw open the door, got in, slammed it shut, and peeled off, all without looking back. Even once.

Mikey slept with me that night.

The minute Mikey put his new pal Freddie into the crate, he started to howl. Not a cute little puppy yap, but a full-fledged, ear-piercing, alarm-sounding, grown-up beagle yodel from hell. Mikey looked at me with those sad dark blue eyes, the color of the sea at midnight. Just like his father's.

I thought of all the sleepless nights we'd spent crying together in California. Without a puppy.

"Just this one night," I said. "I mean it. Just this one night."

Mikey grinned. "Thanks, Mom."

He pulled the howling puppy from the crate and fell onto the bed laughing as Freddie licked him silly.

I tucked in the pair of them, boy and beagle, and turned off the light.

"Sweet dreams," I said, and retired to my own bed with a book. Shakespeare lay curled up on the floor by the bedroom door, and Isis stretched across the curve of my hip as I lay down.

And now we were five.

chapter four

"A Beagle will accept as much attention as you can offer, and then demand more."

—Roger A. Caras, *Harper's Illustrated Handbook of Dogs*

"I got Mikey a beagle puppy," I told my parents on the phone that night, feeling very pleased with myself. New job, new house, new puppy. I had this single mom thing down. I was hoping for a little praise from the two people whose opinion I most valued.

"You already have a dog," my mother said.

With Mom on one line and Dad on the other, it was unsolicited advice in stereo sound. I rolled my eyes, safe in the knowledge that they couldn't see me do it.

"Yes, I know, but apparently I promised him a puppy if we ever got our own house."

"Uh-huh."

"Beagles are good dogs," my dad said. "I had a beagle mix as a kid on the farm. Trixie. Good dog."

"That's a relief," I said, secretly congratulating myself for getting Mikey the same kind of puppy Dad had as a kid. That had to be a good omen. "I don't know anything about beagles."

"You have to *train* a puppy," my mother warned.

"Good nose," the Colonel continued. "Good hunter." He paused. "Better keep him on a leash, they're roamers. Follow their noses to China if you let them."

"We will. Good to know." I felt a slight panic at the thought of Mikey losing his puppy to the call of the open road. I'd lost my first husband to that same call. Of course, he wasn't a dog. Well, my mother might disagree with me on that.

Dad chuckled. "Yeah, Trixie was always in trouble for wandering over into the neighbor's farm."

"You kept him loose?"

"She was a farm dog," Dad said. "Farm dogs run loose."

Maybe my first husband was a farm dog, too.

"You don't have the time to run around after a puppy," my mother said.

"It's Mikey's puppy, Mom. He's taking care of him."

"Uh-huh."

I went back to the safer subject of Trixie the beagle. "Sounds like Trixie was a great dog, Dad. What happened to her?" I had visions of Trixie as a very old dog, shuffling to the front door of the old farmhouse to greet Dad when he came home on weekends from college. Like in that movie *My Dog Skip.*

"Got shot."

"What?"

"Neighbor shot her."

"But why—"

"Dog wandered onto his property one too many times."

"Paul . . . ," my mother said.

"Well, that's what happened." Dad coughed. "That's why I'm saying, you have to keep a beagle on a leash."

"This is Massachusetts. I don't think people shoot dogs here," I said.

"Hmmph." The Colonel didn't think much of our liberal-minded Commonwealth.

"Although Steve next door did tell me that you have to watch out for duck hunters in late autumn," I said. "They hunt from the little island in the middle of the lake."

"That would be a good spot." The Colonel was a hunter of the first order.

"But it's a small lake, isn't it?" my mother said. "How far is that island from your dock?"

"Not that far," I conceded. "But they're shooting up in the sky at the ducks, right, Dad?"

"Should be."

This was not the reassuring conversation I had hoped it would be. I reminded my folks that it was Christmas at our house this year and said goodbye. I reminded myself to keep Freddie on a leash, and Mikey off the lake during duck season, which was coming right up, and went to sleep.

"Time for puppy homework," I announced to Mikey in the booming tones of a sportscaster the next morning.

Mikey was still in bed, asleep even though it was nearly nine. Now that he was in the seventh grade, officially a middle schooler, he was beginning to sleep more, and accommodate less. "Mom, it's Saturday."

"Your puppy doesn't know that. He needs to go out."

Freddie, curled up in the bend of Mikey's long sweat-suited legs, roused himself with a couple of awkward shakes and pulled himself up on all fours. He stumbled over the covers toward me, tail wagging, then paused for a telltale moment.

"Up," I yelled at Mikey, as I grabbed the peeing puppy and ran for the backyard, a drizzle of urine marking our path. Shakespeare bounded after me, followed by a drowsy Mikey.

I put the puppy down, realizing as I released my hands and his paws hit the grass that I'd forgotten the leash. I leaped forward to scoop him up again, but he was gone. I thought of Trixie, dying of gunshot wounds in a faraway field.

"Go get the leash," I yelled to Mikey. "I'll get him." I ran after the puppy, who had disappeared around the corner of the house. "Shakespeare," I ordered, "find Freddie!"

The big dog looked at me, his Beatle-style bangs obscuring his eyes. He'd shown very little interest in Freddie when we'd brought him home yesterday. A couple of sniffs, a couple of pushes with his nose to show the little guy who was alpha dog, and Shakespeare was done with Freddie. He showed no more interest in the puppy now.

I raced up the rise at the side of the cottage, which was in fact the long mound that covered the septic tank system. Because we lived on a lake, the Title Five rules governing water quality were particularly strict, which is why most of our side yard stood higher than the rest of the property. Shakespeare loved it up here, as it gave him full view of his territory—from the dock on the lake all the way round to the entryway, where we parked the cars and entered the house on the street side.

Freddie stood at the peak of the mound, surveying his new home ground, nose up and tail high. Shakespeare vaulted to that same spot, planting his flag as top dog of our territory, scuttling the puppy across the yard and down the other side of the hill.

"Freddie!" I tore down the septic incline after the runaway beagle, who tumbled down the grassy slope like a tri-colored snowball. He came to a stop at the very bottom, where the road met the lawn.

Mikey burst out the front door, leash in hand. Together we cornered the disoriented puppy. Shakespeare took up the flank position, and Isis appeared suddenly from some unknown hiding place, as she was wont to do, and padded back and forth observing the frenetic goings-on, her tail undulating over her back, as if to say, "All this commotion over a mere canine."

An unsteady Freddie struggled to his feet, surrounded by his new family, human and animal. He cocked his head, ears alert, and regarded us curiously each in turn with those big brown eyes. Then he leaned his sleek little head back, silky ears falling to the side, nose pointing to the heavens, and howled like he was on fire.

Mikey slipped his hands around the yowling hound's neck and clipped on the leash.

"Take him for a walk," I ordered, and went back into the house to clean up the trail of piss that ran from Mikey's bedding to the back door, Shakespeare at my heels.

By the time Mikey got back to the house with Freddie, I'd gathered all the dog books we had in the house and spread them out on the kitchen table. Training books, breed books, general dog care books—a lifetime of reading material supplemented by the many dog-related titles published by my current employer.

"I can't be cleaning up pee and poop every day, Mikey. You need to get serious about training him."

"Freddie didn't *poop*, Mom." Mikey cast me a dark look as he brought the laptop to the table and turned it on. "He just got a little nervous when you barged in on him and woke us up so fast. Puppies pee when they get nervous."

"I see, so somehow this is all *my* fault," I said, as the foul scent of feces began to register in my brain. "What is that smell?" I cast Mikey a darker look. "Where is your dog?"

We found Freddie in the far corner of the living room sniffing his own freshly minted poop on the navy-blue carpet. I hated that carpet. I longed to replace it, and at Freddie's current rate of bodily elimination I'd have to do it sooner rather than later.

"Nice," I said, and turned to go. "Clean it up."

"Mom."

"Your dog, your cleanup," I said over my shoulder as I returned to the kitchen table. "Besides, I already cleaned up the pee."

"The lady at the Puppy Palace said he was housebroken." Mikey pulled some paper towels off the roll on the kitchen counter, grabbed the Windex, and proceeded to remove all trace of Freddie's malodorous transgression.

"Yeah, right." I wondered what else the Puppy Palace people told us that was completely false.

"This was just an *accident*, Mom." Mikey came back to the kitchen with the offending Freddie in his arms. "He just needs to get used to his new home." He placed the puppy in the middle of the room, with a ball and chew toy, both of which the recalcitrant beagle ignored in favor of one of Mikey's stray socks. Freddie gnawed on it happily, tearing out the toe with his sharp little puppy teeth.

"Maybe. But in the meantime I can't have him peeing all over my carpet," I told Mikey as I pulled the slobbery sock from the beagle's mouth. "We're going to have to get a baby gate so we can confine him to the kitchen while we're gone."

"Okay." Mikey moved a couple of moving boxes to serve as a makeshift barrier to the living room. "He can't go anywhere now."

"Good. Now, let's read up on puppies." I tossed Mikey a copy of *The Dog Whisperer.*

Mikey tossed it back. "You read it, Mom. I'm researching beagles online." Given the choice between books and computers, Mikey would choose computers every time. It was a pattern of behavior that worried his book editor mother.

As Mikey logged on, I started flipping through the dog-training manuals. Freddie curled up by Shakespeare, who permitted this impudent cuddling with a regal air of resignation.

"Listen to this, Mom. It's from the American Kennel Club website." Mikey pushed a tumble of brown curls out of his eyes as he leaned over the screen.

Much to my delight, longer hair was fashionable now, and the buzz cut he'd worn through much of elementary school was gone, replaced by the irrepressible locks I'd refused to cut when he was a baby, even though he was often mistaken for a girl. Both my boys had beautiful burnished curls—while Alexis got my skinny straight blond hair. Why men always got the best hair, and the longest eyelashes, not to mention the best pay, remained many of life's great mysteries I had yet to unravel.

"Pay attention, Mom." Mikey rolled his eyes.

My digressions, even when unspoken, were a constant source of irritation for Mikey. He was easily the most left-brained of my children, his right-brained siblings being prone to digressions of their own. I knew that sometimes he thought we were all impossible.

"I'm listening," I said.

"Beagles are happy-go-lucky and friendly, making them a wonderful family pet," read Mikey aloud. "His hunting ability, combined with a merry personality, has made the Beagle one of the most popular dogs in the United States."

"Merry, huh?" I looked over at Freddie, snoring sweetly in the shadow of his Big Papi Shakespeare. "Well, he's merrily peed and pooped all over the house."

"Mom." Mikey continued to read. "Since they lived in packs for hundreds of years, they naturally enjoy the company of other dogs and humans." Mikey paused, watching as even in his sleep the puppy burrowed more deeply into the curve of Shakespeare's belly. "Freddie does like Shakespeare."

"That's true," I said. "But it's unclear how much Shakespeare likes Freddie."

"He likes him just fine," Mikey said. "They're a pack now."

"*We're* a pack now," I said. "And you're the man of the house, the alpha dog."

Mikey smiled. "That's right! I'm the alpha dog!" he said. "The alpha dog of the house is hungry. The alpha dog wants pancakes!" Mikey pounded a clenched fist on the table and began to howl.

A startled Shakespeare lumbered to his feet, knocking Freddie aside. The drowsy little hound slipped on the linoleum and fell, limbs akimbo, paws splayed in all directions, ears inside out. He shook his head as if to clear it, and his floppy ears dropped back into place.

I laughed.

"It's not funny, Mom." Mikey jumped off his chair and scooped up the disoriented pup. "Are you okay, Freddie?" He comforted his new best friend with an Eskimo kiss, then turned to Shakespeare. "Bad dog!"

"Don't blame Shakespeare," I said. "It wasn't his fault. He was just minding the alpha dog." I pointed to the books. "Check out beagles in the breed book while I flap some jacks."

By the time I whipped up a couple dozen pancakes and Mikey had wolfed down the greater share of them, we'd learned a lot about our little furry friend.

Freddie Fact #1: Beagles are hounds—and hounds have been bellowing their way into our hearts for hundreds of years. Hunters first and foremost, they roamed the British Isles in packs long before the Roman Empire. Prized for their superior noses and unparalleled skill as rabbit hunters, beagles came in many shapes and sizes—from wirehaired dogs so tiny hunters could carry them in their coat pockets to long-eared, long-bodied breeds resembling dachshunds and basset hounds. By the 1700s, the hare-tracking hounds fell into two basic groups—the slow-moving, bulky, sonorous Southern beagle and the smaller, livelier, more agile North Country beagle. What they all had in common—the bawling call of the wild which earned them the name beagle, from the Old French *bayer*, "to howl," and *gueule*, "mouth."

"Just what we need," I told Mikey. "A howling mouth."

Freddie Fact #2: The rising popularity of foxhunting—and the subsequent decline of rabbit hunting—nearly spelled the end of the breed. But the baying beagles made a comeback in the 1830s, thanks to the Reverend Philip Honeywood, a parson in Essex, who was the first to breed beagles as we now know them.

Freddie Fact #3: Beagles came to America later that century—and in 1888 the AKC officially recognized the breed. The friendly, sturdy little dogs found a welcome home in the New World, quickly gaining in popularity. This favored status peaked in the 1950s, no doubt fueled by the debut of the world's most celebrated beagle, Snoopy, in Charles Schultz's classic *Peanuts* cartoon strip. Beagles remain one of the top ten most popular breeds today.

"Everybody loves beagles," Mikey said. "That's why Charles Schultz made Snoopy a beagle."

Freddie Fact #4: While the majority of beagles are family pets, they are still valued for their sensitive noses. And not just by hunters. Beagles sniff out termites in buildings, illegal drugs in airports, pests and disease in agricultural products. The most famous of these working beagles belong to the U.S. Department of Agriculture's acclaimed canine inspection team known as the Beagle Brigade.

"See, Mom, beagles are smart, too." Mikey stroked Freddie's genetically superior muzzle. "I bet Freddie's smart, too. Maybe he'll make the Beagle Brigade when he grows up."

Freddie Fact #5: Unfortunately, beagles are also valued for medical research as well; their size and temperament make them ideal for clinical trials. In fact, more beagles are used for experimentation than any other breed of dog.

"Oh my God," I said.

"Does that mean they torture them, Mom?" Mikey buried his head in Freddie's soft fur.

"I don't know, honey."

"Don't worry, Freddie," Mikey said. "I won't let them get you."

Freddie Fact #6: If you think that this professional success means that beagles are easy to train, think again. The same super-scenting ability that enables them to detect everything from rabbits to pharmaceuticals with just a swift snuffle also serves as a significant distraction during instruction. Couple the propensity to follow their noses no matter where it may take them with a stubborn nature, and what you get is a dog completely resistant to the usual reward systems used in training—except the one that speaks directly to his nose and his stomach. Namely, food. For this reason, beagles tend to gain weight easily.

"Great," I said to Mikey. "We're going to be stuck with an overweight, out-of-control demon dog."

Mikey shot me a disdainful look. "I'm taking Freddie for a walk."

"That's good," I said. "Apparently he needs the exercise."

Mikey made a great show of ignoring me. He snapped on Freddie's leash with a flourish and trotted the little hound outside, letting the door slam behind him.

Freddie Fact #7: Expressive and entertaining, beagles maintain a youthful appearance and demeanor even as they age. They are the Peter Pans of the dog world. If you want a dog that stays cheerful and lively throughout his life, consider a beagle.

Cheerful and lively throughout his life. I wondered what that meant in dog years. Obviously our poopy, pissy little puppy was as much of a fixer-upper as the house was. As we were. I guess he'd fit right in.

Shakespeare padded over to me, and pushed at my hand with his cold wet nose. I drew my fingers through his thick topknot, scratching the tops of his shaggy black ears.

"Come on, Shakes, time for us old dogs to go join the young whippersnappers."

Shakespeare danced to the front door, always excited at the prospect of a long walk through the cranberry bogs. I stuck a leash in my pocket, on the off chance that I'd need one for the most well behaved member of our fixer-upper family, and we headed for the bogs.

I would make this work for all of us—one walk at a time.

chapter five

"Your goal is for your puppy to meet a hundred new people by the time she's a hundred days old."

—JENNIFER BRIDWELL, *The Everything Dog Obedience Book*

ALL THE DOG BOOKS MIKEY AND I READ EMPHASIZED THE IMPORTANCE of socializing new puppies. They needed to get used to people, all kinds of people. We understood this, but finding people to participate in the socialization of Freddie proved more difficult than anticipated. We'd just moved; we were strangers in a small town in New England, a place well known for its xenophobia. We lived on an unpaved dead-end road that ran alongside a lake, not exactly a hotbed of social activity. Summer was over; the sun worshippers and boaters and water-skiers and kayakers were all gone. Only the hardiest ducks and the die-hard fishermen could be spotted on the water now.

Mikey had no friends here. Neither did I, really. I had pleasant colleagues at the office, of course, but the company was located half an hour's drive away in another town, and employees drove in from as far north as Boston and as far south as Rhode Island to come to work. My off-again, on-again boyfriend Thurber lived in Winchester, some forty miles away. Many of our new neighbors had dropped by to introduce themselves and welcome us to the neighborhood, but they weren't friends, at least not yet—and only time would tell if they would become friends in the future. The only people who came to the house were tradesmen and the UPS guy.

And Joel. When he realized that I'd gone back to California for the reconciliation that wasn't as much as for the Disney gig, he was very disappointed in me. (And who could blame him? Not I.) He never really entirely forgave me for leaving him for my ex, but he remained my friend anyway. In truth, he held the distinction of being the only man I ever dated who remained my friend after we broke up, which probably says far more about him than it does about me.

Joel could fix anything—except me—and he appeared whenever I needed help around the house. Which was nearly all the time.

He showed up on a Sunday afternoon not long after we got Freddie, ostensibly to help us hang pictures. But when he saw Mikey and me struggling to lay the bathroom stick-on tiles I'd gotten at the hardware store, he waved us aside and got to work. Freddie scampered over to him, and licked his ham-fisted hands.

"Who is this mangy mutt?"

Mikey grinned. "That's Freddie. Isn't he cute?"

"I suppose he is." Joel picked up the puppy by the scruff of his loose-skinned neck and handed him off to Mikey. "Now take him away. We don't want the little guy sticking to the floor."

Mikey laughed, and carried his puppy outside to play. Joel watched them go, then turned to me with a shake of his leonine head. "A puppy? What were you thinking?"

"I promised him, if we ever got a house of our own. . . ."

"Hmmph." Joel frowned. "Like you don't have enough on your plate."

"Yeah, I know." I shrugged. "But Mikey's so happy."

"I guess." Joel dropped to his knees and started to glue the tiles to the floor. Isis ran into the bathroom after him, rubbing her lithe frame against his folded thighs. Joel was one of her favorite humans; she knew that while Joel didn't mind dogs, he was really a cat person at heart. He didn't shoo the kitty away, but stroked her soft tiger fur and tickled her chin as she purred with increasing pleasure.

I left the two of them alone and went into the kitchen to make meatloaf and mashed potatoes. Whenever Joel did work around the house, I paid him back in meatloaf. The man loved my meatloaf. It was the least I could do.

The floor finished, Joel left right after dinner. We all walked out to the front deck, where I gave the man my mother thought I should have married a hug goodbye. As Joel turned to go, in a quick move that surprised us all, Mikey threw himself at the big guy, wrapping his long skinny arms around Joel's thick strong trunk. My son held on to my former boyfriend for a long time.

"You're coming back soon, right?" asked Mikey, as he reluctantly stepped away from Joel.

"Sure."

"Next Sunday?"

"We'll see how the week goes."

"Okay."

"Take good care of that puppy."

"Sure." Mikey beamed.

Mikey waved, and then disappeared into the house after Freddie. I stayed out on the deck in the growing darkness, watching as Joel climbed into his Jeep and headed down our pond-side road to Route 14, his personalized "Oregon" plates proclaiming his undying loyalty to his home state. I knew what Mikey didn't: that Joel would only be back next Sunday if Thurber weren't around.

I met Thurber while I was living in Salem, after we escaped from California—and after Joel told me he was glad I was safely back in Massachusetts, but that friendship was all he could offer me now.

So I joined an online dating site, determined to put all of my exes behind me, Joel included. "James Thurber Seeking Dorothy Parker" read his headline on his profile. How could I, a die-hard Parker fan, possibly resist that? A sucker punch right to my overactive imagination.

I costumed very carefully for our first date that cold damp March evening in 2002. A little black velvet dress worthy of a Dorothy Parker poem, matching coat, and a saucy cranberry cloche bedecked with a silk rose. I dressed for fireworks—and I wasn't disappointed.

A literary match made in heaven, I thought when I met him for the first time in the small dark bar of my favorite restaurant in Salem. Thurber was tall and handsome and funny and just enough younger than I to make me feel hip and naughty. Vaguely professorial in his tweed jacket and jeans, the lanky Yankee peppered his speech with erudite *bons mots* and clever ripostes and self-deprecating witticisms guaranteed to tickle my intellectual fancy.

We drank martinis, quoting our favorite Parker poem—the one about the dangerous consequences of drinking too many martinis—and nearly ended up under the table ourselves. It was the night before my forty-second birthday and he presented me with a copy of Thurber's *Men and Dogs*, the edition with the foreword by Dorothy Parker.

I was smitten—and not in a good way.

When my parents came to visit me two weeks later, I told my mother privately that unless Thurber turned out to be a real jerk, I was going to marry him.

"You don't need a husband," she said.

"Nobody *needs* a husband, Mom." I sighed in pleasure as I took in Thurber across the room talking to my father. "But everybody *wants* one."

"You've *been* married," Mom said loudly, her eyebrows arching in displeasure. "Twice."

"Put your eyebrows down, Mom." I pulled her into the kitchen where we could be alone. "Listen, I know what you're thinking." I paused.

My mother looked at me as if to say, *You never really know what I'm thinking.* Which was often true, given my mother's inscrutable reserve. But not this time.

I began again. "*Sweet Mother of God*, you're thinking, *there she goes again.*" I threw up my hands in mock exasperation. "*She barely knows the guy and she's already thinking marriage—as if two husbands weren't enough for anybody.*" I paused again. "But this would be different. *He's* different."

"Uh-huh," my mother said.

I knew what she was thinking again this time, too. *You sure can pick 'em*, which was what the Colonel always said whenever the subject of my marriages came up.

"He is *different*," I insisted, answering my father's unspoken criticism for both of us.

Thurber couldn't have been more different from my second husband, the lean, good-looking Irishman who wore his blue-collar status like a badge of honor. Or my first husband, the Jewish New Yorker who was crazy brilliant—emphasis on the crazy. Thurber was a Mayflower New Englander with the cultured manner and writerly air of John Updike. A man who spoke as easily with bartenders about the Red Sox as he spoke with professors about literature. A man who quoted Seinfeld as easily as he quoted Shakespeare. A man who happily watched *Masterpiece Theatre* with me and read *The New York Times Book Review* with me and danced to Neil Youngs's *Harvest Moon* with me. These were small things, to be sure, but things that nonetheless meant the world to me—things that neither of my exes had ever cared to share with me. For the first time in my life I felt that a man understood me—and appreciated me for who I really was.

I was thinking: *Where else on earth would I find a man who'd nickname me Parker?*

What I was not thinking was: *What fresh hell is this?*

Over the next two years, fresh hell would come and go a couple of times. Thurber was a charming guy who truly loved me, but one whose extreme emotionalism complicated his life—and mine. We had come close to marrying more than once, but each time Thurber got cold feet—and when he did, I broke up with him. When I broke up with him, he went out with other women, some of whom did not give up easily when we inevitably reconciled and lingered longer than they should have. There were tears and shouts, middle-of-the-night phone calls and unexpected knocks at the door, accusations and apologies.

Thurber seemed to feed on this drama, and once upon a time that would have been true for me as well. But I'd exhausted the emotional energy required to maintain this fever pitch long ago on my ex-husbands. For the first time in my life, I understood why men complained about women who always wanted to share their feelings and talk about their relationship. That's what Thurber always wanted to do—and all I wanted to do was drink martinis, go to the movies, and get laid. Not necessarily in that order.

When I got the job on the South Shore and started house hunting, we had just reconciled after yet another breakup. We had planned to move in together, but this time I was the one who got cold feet. I rationalized my hesitation: the cottage was small, after all, barely big enough for me and Mikey, and certainly not big enough for the *Sturm und Drang* that often characterized Life with Thurber. He was pushing for me to make a commitment, and I was stalling.

The weekend after Joel finished the bathroom floor, Thurber came to visit us from Arlington, the suburb outside Boston where he lived. Thurber didn't have a car; he was one of those Boston boys who claimed that a car was more of a nuisance than a benefit. To get to Lytton from Arlington wasn't easy; Thurber had to change trains three times on the ninety-minute journey from his studio apartment to my little cottage. This, coupled with our on-again, off-again pattern, meant that we hadn't seen much of each other since I'd moved south.

I picked Thurber up at the train station and he slipped into my car and into my arms once more.

"Here," he said to me in between kisses. Which was his way of saying that he belonged here with me.

"Here," I answered.

When the windows started to steam over, I pulled myself away, and drove him to the house. I gave him the grand tour of the tiny cottage, and we stopped out back on the dock by the water. The trees were in full color now, rimming the lake with gold and red reflections.

"It's beautiful here." Thurber started toward me, but a door slammed behind us. We turned to watch Shakespeare and Freddie bounding down the slope to the dock, a distraught Mikey in hot pursuit.

"Catch him, Mom!"

The little beagle's bullet-shaped body lent him a surprising speed—if and when he had a direct destination in mind. That is, if he knew where he was going. And he knew where he was going; he was going wherever the big dog went. Ears flying like sails, the puppy darted down the steps and across the patio after Shakespeare. The long-legged Shakespeare cantered gracefully to the edge of the patio where the water lapped at the concrete ridge, and slipped onto the wooden dock as sleekly as a gazelle. He made a quick, hard stop just short of the end of the dock, where Thurber and I stood.

Freddie, on the other hand, did not stop at the finish line, but kept on running, scampering right off the dock and into the lake.

"Freddie!" Mikey dashed down the dock, screaming. "Mom, do something!"

I jumped into the chilly green water after the dog, ruining yet another pair of the inappropriate high heels I refused to give up even though I now officially lived in the country. But Thurber had already slid down to his knees and drawn a large languorous hand under the flailing Freddie, fishing him out of the water like an old boot. The squirming bundle of wet fur shook violently—and howled even harder. Thurber held the dripping dog firmly with both hands now, arms outstretched, while Freddie twisted and turned.

"Why don't you go get a towel for Freddie," Thurber said to Mikey. "And maybe one for your mom, too."

"Not the good ones!" I yelled after Mikey, as he tore up the slope to the house. I shook my head. "He's going to get the good ones." I sighed, and waited for Thurber to help me out. But apparently Freddie's distress outranked mine. I glared at them both. "This water is cold, you know."

"Sorry." Thurber tucked Freddie under his left arm like the squealing little pig he resembled at this moment. "I was busy saving the dog." He offered me his right hand, steadying my ascent as I pulled my spiky, messy pumps out of the muddy lake bottom and clambered back onto the dock.

He ran his eyes down my wet jean-clad legs to my feet and the muck-splattered, soggy high heels that covered them. "Not sure I can save the shoes."

I pulled them off just as Mikey returned with the towels. The taupe Egyptian cotton ones I paid way too much for, even on sale. "Those are the *good* towels."

"It's an emergency, Mom!" Mikey wrapped the thick terrycloth around Freddie, tucking it around and under his shivering body while Thurber held him tight.

"Ahem," I said. "Excuse me!"

Mikey threw the other towel at me without a second glance. I dried my legs off while I watched Thurber calm the bedraggled Freddie. I was a sucker for a man who was good with animals.

Thurber had always loved Shakespeare and Isis—and they loved him back. Freddie was no different, taking to his new savior right away. The dog was warm and happy in his arms. I knew just how he felt.

"He's a great puppy," Thurber told Mikey as he rubbed the sweet spot between Freddie's ears. "Congratulations."

"Yeah." Mikey grabbed his damp little dog around his sturdy middle and pulled him away from Thurber.

"Careful," Thurber admonished. "You don't want to hurt him. Puppies are fragile."

"I know what I'm doing."

"Really?" I said. "Your puppy just nearly drowned."

Mikey looked from me to Thurber and back again, frowning. It was hard to tell which of us he loathed more. "Beagles can swim, Mom."

"Really?" I asked again. "Then why the panic?"

Mikey regarded me as if I were a single-celled amoeba. "It was his first time in the lake, Mom."

"Mikey, thank Thurber for rescuing your dog."

"Yeah, whatever."

Those were fighting words. "Michael Paul."

"I don't know what *he's* doing here, anyway." Mikey stomped away from us, Freddie held closely to his chest, head buried in his puppy's soft moist coat.

"That's nice," I hollered after my rude son. "Sorry," I said to Thurber.

Thurber shrugged and stooped to pet Shakespeare, who'd appeared at his side for a little head scratch as soon as the annoying puppy had gone. "At least the dogs like me."

"I like you, too." I kissed him. And he kissed me back.

"Okay, okay," I said, answering the question that hung between us. "Start packing."

Thurber kissed me again. "Thanks, Parker."

Hand in hand, Shakespeare at our heels, we started back up to the cottage.

"He's not going to like my moving in," Thurber said.

"Don't worry," I said. "He'll come around."

To celebrate buying a house and getting a puppy and reconciling with Thurber, we decided to throw a big housewarming party. Thurber and I designed the invitations together and sent them out to all of our old Salem friends, my new colleagues on the South Shore, our new lake neighbors, and Thurber's family and friends, most of whom he'd known since childhood. It was the first party we ever planned together; I couldn't help but think of it as a sort of dress rehearsal for the wedding we might have in the spring.

"I'll make my award-winning chili," I said. "You can make your special margaritas."

"Fine," said Thurber, "but when we get married next May, we'll have lobster and martinis."

I laughed. "One celebration at a time."

"What about hot dogs and cheeseburgers?" asked Mikey. "We need hot dogs and cheeseburgers for my friends."

"Of course," I said, thrilled that Mikey now actually had friends.

Not only did Mikey have a new puppy to show off at the party, he also had a new friend, a boy his age from down the street named Louie. Louie was a foster child who lived with Bill, a single father who took in foster kids now that his own children were nearly grown. Louie was the only boy Mikey's age on our street, so I was thrilled that they'd become buddies. Now Louie showed up every morning at 6 A.M. for breakfast with me and Mikey. After chowing down on whatever I happened to have on hand—Louie preferred Cheerios and donuts to oatmeal and raisin bread—he and Mikey would then walk together to the bus stop at the end of the road.

Louie was coming to the party, along with his foster brothers. There would be other kids, too, mostly the children of my friends and colleagues. I told Mikey he could ask some of the boys on his soccer team, but he demurred.

"They're all dorks," Mikey said.

Which I knew was junior high–speak for *I haven't made any friends on the soccer team yet.*

"I see," I said.

Which he knew was mom-speak for *I could say something here but I will refrain for both our sakes.*

Mikey played goalie for a junior-high soccer team here in Lytton, just as he had back in Salem. I took Freddie and Shakespeare with me to the games; all the little kids on the sidelines played with the lively pup with the buttery brown ears and the fast-forward tail while Shakespeare guarded me as I cheered Mikey on. But even Freddie couldn't help Mikey feel like a true member of the team.

"We need a Weber," I said, changing the subject. "A Weber is—"

"I know what a Weber is, Mom."

Of course he did, I thought, cursing myself and my ex at the same time. His father was a big Weber fan. *The only grill worth having*, he'd told me when he brought one home not long after we were married. In my ex's world, real men didn't cook, they grilled. Mikey probably helped his father fire up the Weber grill every night of every summer back in California, where he spent most of school vacation with his dad. At *her* house.

"I have other plans," said my ex, when he left me and Mikey stranded at the condo in San Tadeo that terrible day we moved across the country to be a family again. And as every woman knows, "I have other plans" nearly always means *I have another woman.* I understood that, even then, but I never understood what that had to do with Mikey. Having another woman meant abandoning me—*not* Mikey. His father had always exercised his visitation rights to the fullest extent; he'd insisted on it. He'd always gone out of his way to see his son, no matter how far the physical distance between them. He may have not paid child support regularly, but he always paid for airline tickets to fly Mikey back and forth for visitation, even when he was dead broke. He'd actively maintained a close relationship with his son regardless of his circumstances, good or bad. At the time I simply couldn't imagine the woman who could come between Mikey and his dad.

Now, four years later, I knew better.

I am a tall blonde named Paula. The woman my ex had dumped me and Mikey for in San Tadeo was a tall blonde named . . . well, let's just say her name began with a *P* and was close enough to mine to invite endless comparisons, jokes, and puns among mutual friends and family. You and I may readily see the Freudian implications here—but my ex did not. I would have thought it hilarious, a back-handed compliment of ironic proportions, if I hadn't been so devastated—especially when he married her not long afterwards, in a big country club wedding written up in the society pages of the *San Tadeo Chronicle*.

My ex was married, and Mikey and I were stuck in California, unwilling witnesses to my ex's new life. In time, my devastation degraded into just being pissed off. How dare he get on with his life with another blonde with (half of) my name! How dare he be happy with half-name P! How dare he be happy with anyone besides me, even women whose first names did not begin with *P*!

But Mikey's attitude toward his new stepmother was far more complicated. My ex lived in *her* house with *her* boys according to *her* rules—and Mikey felt that difference keenly. He never felt quite good enough there, a feeling reinforced by what we saw as her favoring of her boys and her disapproval of Mikey.

Over time, these little indignities added up. She took my ex and her boys and Mikey's older half-sister (from his father's first marriage) on a family vacation to Hawaii—but left Mikey at home with me. ("We didn't ask your mom because we knew she'd say no," his stepbrother told him later. As if I would ever deny any child of mine a trip to Hawaii. As my ex well knew, my older children had gone on several trips to Hawaii with their dad, and I never said no to those trips, even though their father owed me hundreds of thousands of dollars in back child support.)

She made him accompany his stepbrothers to summer school, even though Mikey was a good student with no need for remedial instruction. (The next summer I wrote a letter to my ex on Mikey's behalf asking that he be allowed to go to camp instead, but that request was denied.) She sent him to manners school because he wasn't as "well-mannered" as her boys. (I dubbed her Miss Priss after that, and the name stuck.)

Per our custody agreement, Mikey spent holidays and most of summer vacation with his dad at Miss Priss's house year in and year out, like it or not. When he first came back from these visits, he was often upset and angry, and would recall not-so-fondly what went on while he stayed with his dad.

But within a couple of days of coming home, Mikey's good nature would reassert itself. All his references to California would cease, and we would pretend the Golden State didn't exist. Mikey would then avoid all mention of his father.

Mikey didn't mention his father now as we discussed the Weber, either. Neither did I. His father hung in the air between Mikey and me, quieting us both. An awkward stillness set in.

"Let's go get the grill, Mom," Mikey said, effectively ending our silence and changing the course of our conversation lest it veer west without warning.

Thirty minutes later, we were back from Rocky's Hardware with the classic black Weber, charcoal, lighter fluid, a box of long-handled fireplace matches, and a full set of stainless steel grilling utensils. Thurber was on his way back to Arlington. He'd be back in two weeks, the weekend of the open house.

"We need to try the Weber out, Mom," Mikey said. "*Before* the party."

"Good idea." I sat at the picnic table, keeping one eye on Freddie and the water's edge and the other on Mikey as he set up the briquettes in a careful pyramid, just as his father used to do. He replaced the cooking grid, poured on the lighter fluid, and struck a match, lighting the coals in a blast of flames. At the *whoosh* of the initial blaze, Freddie scampered over to Mikey, tail high, nose down, as if he knew that fire sooner or later equaled meat.

"Now we need to wait for the coals to get hot, Mom." Mikey spoke with the same fierce assurance his father did. "It'll be about thirty, forty minutes." He picked up his puppy and came over to sit by me at the table, Freddie on his lap.

"He's going to move in with us, isn't he?"

"Maybe," I said, knowing he meant Thurber.

Mikey shot me a "get real" look.

"Probably," I conceded.

Mikey scowled.

"I don't know why you're being this way," I told him. "He's always very nice to you."

"He makes you cry."

He had me there.

"Well, yes, from time to time, he does." I ruffled my son's curls, and he ducked. "But you know what a crybaby I am." I'd been known to cry at school plays, soccer games, and sunsets—not to mention museums, most national holidays, and the occasional Hallmark commercial.

Mikey laughed at me. "Yeah."

"I could cry right now, watching Freddie lick your face."

Mikey shook his head. "You need to go get the hamburger."

I jumped to my feet, and saluted the King of the Grill. "Yes, sir!"

I thought about Thurber and Mikey as I rolled out the patties. I wanted this to work; I couldn't bear a repeat of my ex and my older kids. When we got married, we brought together his daughter and my two kids—and then added Mikey, who belonged to us all. I'd expected a modern-day blended family version of *The Brady Bunch*. What I'd gotten was the Stepfamily from Hell. Alexis and Greg never wanted a stepfather, never mind a stepfather like him. A man as different from their father as the man in the moon. And just as unyielding.

But like I told my mother, this would be different. Thurber had never been cold or hard or angry with Mikey. He was warm and flexible and amenable, at least most of the time. Everything would be just fine. We would be just fine.

I placed the raw patties on a platter and headed down to the grill, where both Mikey and Freddie waited expectantly for me.

Or, rather, the beef.

We could make this work, I thought, as I watched Mikey flip the burgers, much to Freddie and Shakespeare's delight and frustration. After all, what a boy really needed was a good home, a mother who loved him, and a good male role model. Mikey would have all that with me and Thurber on the lake. *Plus* a puppy who worshipped him.

What could possibly go wrong?

chapter six

"Apparently dogs believe that if something fits into their mouths, then it is food, no matter what it tastes like."

—STANLEY COREN, *How to Speak Dog*

I T WAS FRIDAY NIGHT. THE OPEN HOUSE WAS ON SUNDAY. AFTER DINNER, Mikey settled down with *Star Wars Battlefront* and his Xbox, Freddie on his lap, and I drove to the train station to pick up Thurber. We agreed that he would spend the whole weekend with us to help prepare for the party—thinking of it as a sort of dry run for moving in. Thurber already had some of his things at the house, but if all went well this weekend he'd be moving in more of his stuff over the course of the next month.

The train station was in the next town over, about five miles away. The commuter rail only ran every hour or so at this time of night. Thurber was due on the 9:13 P.M. train from South Station in Boston, the third leg of his journey from Arlington. I pulled into the lot right on schedule, at 9:10, just a couple of minutes early. I drove the car to the pickup section, up front alongside the tracks. I heard the whistle blow, and smiled. I loved the romance of meeting Thurber at the train station; the Forties-style "Who Knows Where, Who Knows When" quality about it completely entranced me.

The train pulled into the station with a rush of cold air and the squeal of brakes. I watched in the rear-view mirror as the travelers debarked: a couple of college students in jeans and Boston University T-shirts; a businessman in a dark suit and overcoat; a middle-aged nurse in scrubs coming home after a long shift. I imagined the lives of these passengers, picturing them at work, at home, at the grocery store. I made up lovers for them, gave them children and grandchildren, sent them on trips to Disney World and Europe. I wondered who was picking them up or how far they had to drive home.

More people got off—and a few got on. Thurber was not among them. I checked my phone for messages, but no one had called. I dialed his number, but the line went straight to voice mail.

The platform was empty now. I sat there in silence as the train chugged away slowly. Thurber was not coming. He was not answering my calls, or calling me to explain his absence.

Out of all the scenarios I had imagined, I had not imagined this one. I waited another five minutes, and then started the car and headed for home.

Alone.

"Where is he?" Mikey asked without taking his eyes off the digital *Star Wars* stormtroopers when I came home sans Thurber.

"He's not coming." I collapsed onto the couch next to Mikey, going through the contents of my liquor cabinet in my mind, searching for the perfect libation to ease the pain spreading through the pores of my skin and invading the corpuscles of my body and flooding the arteries of my heart. Beer? *Too tame.* Wine? *Too civilized.* Gin? *Perfect.* I would have one perfect martini—just one.

"Why not?"

"Unclear." I sighed. "Try not to look so happy about it."

Mikey paused his game, making the ultimate sacrifice in the name of his mother's suffering. "It's Friday night. *Numb3rs* night."

Every Friday night my little math genius and I celebrated the beginning of the weekend by watching *Numb3rs* together. This was one of the many little mother/son rituals that marked our life together. We both drew a small measure of comfort from these homey rituals, but over time and trauma the solace we gained added up to a sweet if small life. I smiled.

"I'll make the popcorn," I said. *And a martini.*

It was during this critical weekly tradition that we made two discoveries that would ultimately change everything: 1) Thurber would not be making his special margaritas at the open house, and 2) Freddie loved popcorn.

Normally we didn't share our popcorn with the animals. Shakespeare had never shown much interest in it; he was much too well mannered to beg for food. He depended on the kindness of humans for his treats—with far better luck than Blanche DuBois. Isis would no more deign to dine on corn—food for swine, as all cats were born knowing—than she would deign to dine on any food other than Deli-Cat (dry) and Fancy Feast (wet). The exceptions being tuna right from the can and the boiled organ meats from the turkey that graced our table every year at Thanksgiving dinner.

Freddie, on the other hand, had shown a great hunger for virtually every conceivably edible object in the house. I placed the popcorn bowl down on the sofa between Mikey and me, and we tuned in to *Numb3rs.* Shakespeare lay on his round bed across the room, content. Freddie abandoned his matching doggie pillow and dashed to the couch. He dove for the bowl in a surprisingly graceful arc—and landed muzzle down smack in the middle of it. Yellow puffs fluttered to the floor; hard unpopped kernels pinged the hardwood. Freddie munched and crunched and chomped, his little jaws shaking with joy.

"Off the couch!" I pushed the popcorn-consuming deviant little hound head over paws down to the ground and grabbed the bowl. "Off the couch!"

"Mom! You're hurting him!" Mikey pulled at the perplexed puppy, who however unsteady on his feet was not so disoriented he couldn't scarf up the popcorn on the floor. Freddie sucked up the fallen forbidden fruit like an errant vacuum cleaner gone wild. Mikey pulled harder, but the stubborn little glutton held fast, thick paws braced against the floorboards. Finally Mikey's superior strength won out, propelling the squirming puppy onto his lap. Mikey held him on his back, bloated stomach exposed, and scratched the dog's belly. Freddie relaxed, belly scratching being the one thing he liked nearly as much as food.

"Easy, buddy," I advised my son. "He swallowed that popcorn whole and if you're not careful, you'll be cleaning up projectile vomiting any minute."

"Gross, Mom."

"I'm just saying . . . ." My voice trailed off as I deposited the bowl on the kitchen table and retrieved a handheld broom and dustpan from under the sink.

I was still on my knees sweeping up the remains of the popcorn, what little the puppy had somehow missed, when the phone began to ring and Freddie began to puke.

"Take him outside," I yelled to Mikey. *"Now."*

My son ran for the back door, Freddie in hand, leaving a trail of throw-up in his wake. I stumbled to my feet and fished my cell from my purse just as the call went to voice mail. I didn't recognize the number, so I put the phone down while I fetched the paper towels and the Windex. Mikey came back inside with Freddie.

"Are you sure that he's finished?"

Mikey shrugged. "Guess so."

"Okay, why don't you calm him down and get him in his bed? It's past his bedtime. I'll deal with the mess."

"Thanks, Mom." Mikey gave me a sheepish look.

I went back to the kitchen and listened to the voice mail. It was Thurber, saying that he would be coming by early the next day to get his stuff. He knew that Mikey had a soccer game in the morning, so he planned to come while we were gone and no one was home.

I couldn't believe it. He was dumping me, dumping us, dumping our future together—no excuses, no apologies, no explanations. Just a notice that he'd be invading my home to retrieve his belongings.

Call me unreasonable, but I didn't want him in my house when I wasn't there. Thurber had no car, so that meant someone would be driving him. Someone I didn't know, in my house, along with Thurber, whom I didn't want in my house, either. I called him back, at the unknown number listed on the phone. The phone rang several times; no one answered. The call went to voice mail; I listened to a recording by a breathy woman named Alyssa, who asked me to please leave a message. She'd get back to me.

I bet she would. At the tone I cleared my throat and began to speak. "This is Paula calling for Thurber. You need to call me to arrange pickup of your things. Dropping by while I am not here is not acceptable. Thank you."

Alyssa was a shrink from Schenectady. She had called me once before, on Thurber's behalf. That was during our last big breakup, when Mikey and I were still living in Salem, before we moved into our cottage on the South Shore. *Alyssa.* He'd met her through some singles organization, and they'd become friendly. Alyssa was a therapist, Thurber told me, who was helping him sort out his feelings. *Again with the feelings*, I thought.

That time, Alyssa called me to explain that Thurber loved me, and that I should take him back. She didn't understand why I was so angry with Thurber for trying to reconcile with me even as he was seeing someone else. I wondered just how good a therapist she could be. *Again with the other women.*

This time, Alyssa was coming to my house to help him break up with me. She probably didn't understand why I was so angry with Thurber about that either. I worried for the woman's patients. *Again with the Sturm und Drang.*

I slipped the phone back into my purse, and made myself that martini. Then I retrieved the paper towels and Windex, and wiped up the vomit. When all was shipshape once more, I sat down on the couch, martini in hand.

Mikey was across the room, stroking his sleeping puppy as he lay curled up on his doggy bed. "He's asleep now, Mom. I think all that barfing wore him out."

"Good," I said, patting the sofa seat. "Come on. Back to *Numb3rs*."

Mikey joined me, and we cuddled up together. We settled down to watch the rest of the show, fighting over the lap blanket. Mikey ended up with most of it, as he always did, and fell asleep on the couch before the episode ended.

When *Numb3rs* was over, I helped the drowsy boy and his puppy to bed. Then I made myself another martini, and slipped outside with Shakespeare. It was a cool, clear night on the lake, the kind where the stars shone bright against the dark autumn sky. No sign yet of the rain forecast for the morrow. I sat on the stone steps leading down to the dock, staring out at the nearly full moon shining on the water. Shakespeare sat at my feet, facing toward me, and gently laid his big shaggy black head on my knee. I rubbed his dark topknot, soft as fleece, with my right hand, and sipped the cold gin with my left.

I didn't cry.

I didn't yell.

I didn't feel.

I just wondered if and when I'd ever find a good man with whom to share this beautiful view.

The next morning dawned cold and wet, the storm moving in from the Great Lakes. Mikey and his puppy slept in while I ran around the house, preparing for the open house. We'd been in the house for nearly two months now, but there was still so much left to do. Usually thanks to my Army brat training by this time I'd have been completely moved in, but the demands of the new job coupled with Mikey's school and soccer activities had interfered with my military approach to new quarters. Determined to make up for lost time, I turned on John Mellencamp—the best beat to unpack by—and got busy. I unpacked the last of the moving boxes, hung pictures and arranged furniture, dusted and vacuumed and de-cluttered. Anything I found that belonged to Thurber, I threw in a box intended for the front deck. After two hours of nonstop activity, the place didn't look half bad. I was pleased, pleased with my little cottage, pleased with my little life. Who needed a man? More to the point, who needed Thurber?

The phone rang and I answered it, knowing it would be Thurber. "Yes?"

"Is this Paula?" asked Alyssa, the shrink from Schenectady with the breathy voice.

I panicked and hung up. The phone rang again within seconds. The woman must have me on speed dial. This time it was Thurber.

"Parker—"

"Don't call me that. What's wrong with your phone?"

"It died. So I had to borrow a friend's."

"Right." I inhaled deeply, and exhaled loudly. "Your things will be in a box outside. If you're not here by 2 P.M. to get them, I'll give it all to Goodwill."

"It's raining." Thurber spoke with a sharp impatience that managed to call my intelligence into question.

"Not my problem," I snapped back. I counted to ten in every language I knew. *One, two, three* . . . .

"I'll come after you're gone. It would be easier for everyone that way."

"That would be trespassing." I paused. *Uno, dos, tres* . . . . "This is my house, not yours."

"I have a key."

"Obviously a mistake on my part." *Un, deux, trois* . . . . "Leave it under the pot of red geraniums on the front deck step."

"But—"

"Look, you are not welcome here. *She* is not welcome here." *Eins, zwei, drei* . . . . "You can pick up your stuff outside before I leave for Mikey's game, or forfeit it."

"You don't have the right to do that."

I was out of numbers. "And if that woman sets foot on my property, I'm calling the police."

As the time for us to leave for Mikey's game grew closer, and Thurber did not appear, I grew nervous. I arranged for Mikey to get a ride to the game with his teammate Jacob.

"I'll be there as soon as I can," I promised as I walked him out in the cold drizzle to his ride. Jacob's mom Alice was driving.

"Thanks, Alice."

"No problem." Alice looked at me. She was a cute petite brunette, one of those tidy women who led a tidy life: husband, house, kids. The kind of secure, ordered existence that had thus far eluded me. I wondered if her husband, Gary, had ever called her from another woman's phone.

Alice was still looking at me. "Is everything all right?"

"Yes, fine," I said. "I just need to take care of a couple of things here."

Mikey climbed in. "You never missed a game before, Mom."

"I know. I'm sorry," I said. "Put on your seatbelt." I shut the car door.

"Thanks again," I said to Alice.

Mikey rolled down the window and stuck out his head to yell at me as Alice backed up her Jeep. "This has to do with him, right?"

"I'm taking care of it," I told my son.

"Get rid of him, Mom." Mikey held his thumb and index finger up to his forehead in the classic "L is for Loser" configuration.

I shook my head. "Not nice."

"But so true!" Mikey shouted as the car started down the road.

I watched them drive away and then went into the house to call the police. This was a small town, with very little crime, so I knew they wouldn't be too busy on a rainy Saturday morning. I explained the circumstances and asked if I could get a restraining order to keep Thurber and Alyssa out of my house while I was gone.

But apparently that would only be possible if there were the "threat of harm." Nonetheless, the police agreed to check it out. I gave them Alyssa's number, and then popped in and out of the shower. I threw on some decent clothes and fixed my face. I switched out John Mellencamp for Janis Joplin, cranked up the volume, and went back to cleaning, apron on.

Thirty minutes later, a police car pulled into my driveway. A dark blue Honda station wagon with New York plates followed. From my kitchen window, I watched a tall, pale, freckled uniformed cop in his thirties exit his vehicle and walk toward the house. I pulled off the apron and stepped out on the deck to meet him. I shook the officer's hand, introducing myself and thanking him for coming.

"I'll go get his stuff," I said.

By the time I dragged the box out to the front deck, Thurber was standing there next to the police officer.

"Is that all of it?" asked the police officer.

"Yes," I said.

"I'd like to look for myself," Thurber said, as if he were on a local garden tour.

"That's all there is," I repeated, addressing the police officer, not Thurber.

"What about the garage?" Thurber addressed this question to me. I didn't even look at him. "He may have more stuff in the garage."

"Can he go look in there?" the officer asked. "I'll be with him."

"Okay," I conceded.

Thurber and the officer disappeared by the side door into the garage. Thurber came out a few moments later, arms full of the clothes I'd forgotten that he'd stored in a freestanding closet in a far corner of the garage. Alyssa got out of the Honda now and opened the hatchback. Her breathy voice didn't match the woman I saw out in the road. She was tall and lumpy, or maybe it was just the unflattering sweats she was wearing. She wore no makeup and was having a very bad hair day. I smiled, and asked God to forgive me as I congratulated myself on taking the time to put on a little mascara and lip-gloss and change into clean jeans and a deep V-necked sweater that showed just a hint of cleavage.

Alyssa plodded around the station wagon in old sneakers, headed for the walkway that led to my front door.

"Hey!" The word just slipped out of my mouth, and I hurled it like an accusation.

Thurber and the cop stopped short. Alyssa the clueless shrink from Schenectady kept on walking.

I lowered my voice to a growl. "I don't want her on my property."

"Oh please." Thurber's voice held that exasperated tone men reserve for hysterical women.

I appealed to the police officer. "I don't *know* her."

He nodded and turned to Alyssa. "Ma'am, I'm going to have to ask you to stay inside your vehicle."

I stood with my back up against the front door for support as I watched Thurber finish loading her car. Freddie and Shakespeare were on the other side of the door; I could hear Freddie crying and scratching at the door.

What next? I thought as Thurber slipped into the passenger seat of the Honda and she drove them away.

"I think we're good to go," the freckle-faced officer said to me. "You might want to change those locks."

"Yes. Of course."

"You're better off without him," he said.

I nodded, unable to speak. I shook his hand again. Pumped it up and down. Up and down. Up and down. "Thank you so much."

"Yes, ma'am." The officer withdrew his hand carefully and retreated.

As soon as he left, I snapped the leashes on Freddie and Shakespeare, piled them all into the Kia, and headed for Mikey's soccer game. This game was in a town some thirty minutes away, farther west and best reached on back roads. It was slow going, due to the slick streets and the Saturday traffic.

By the time I got to the soccer field, it was raining hard, a wintry bitter rain that got under your skin and chilled you to the bone. The kids were cold and dirty and miserable, their knees and shins marked with gray-brown streaks of grime. Neither team had scored; the soccer field was slick with rain and mud, as was the ball. They should have called the game, but I knew from experience that hardly ever happened.

There were no bleachers at this field. Fortified against the elements in a hooded raincoat, I sat in one of the folding beach chairs I kept in the car for just such occasions, the dogs by my side. Shakespeare parked as much of his large furry body as possible under my seat, regarding me with a forlorn look. He hated the rain; once wet, his thick, sheepdog's coat took hours to dry.

Freddie, on the other hand, loved the rain. Usually he played with the small children who accompanied their parents to their siblings' soccer games, but today the rain kept all the sensible parents in their cars, watching the game through their windshields, wipers flying. So he played by himself, pouncing on the puddles, rolling in the mire, slipping in the sludge. I had him on one of those long retractable leashes so I wouldn't have to chase around after him in the downpour. Which meant that the rambunctious pup had plenty of legroom, some twenty feet of it. But as I was learning, there was never quite enough room to roam for Freddie. He pulled on the leash at the edge of the sidelines, bright brown eyes on the boys as they scuttled about the field.

Just as the rain shower morphed into a full-throttle torrent, Freddie tugged too hard—and the lead snapped. Freddie tore off across the lawn toward the boys on the field, hitting a patch of gravel and pitching a long spray of wet pebbles in his wake. Some of which managed to ping my kneecaps.

"Freddie!" I scrambled to my feet, slipping in my boots, their medium-high, mere two-inch heels my only concession to the weather and the venue. I fell to my pebbled knees, the damp ground staining my new jeans with soil and grass. I swore, and then cursed myself for swearing. This was, after all, a family event. But my obscene slip went unnoticed; everyone stayed in their cars, apparently unmoved by Freddie's sudden flight and my subsequent plight.

I tossed the broken leash to the ground, unsnapped the long red strap attached to Shakespeare's collar, and hightailed it for the field. Loyal Shakespeare shambled to his feet and followed me none too happily into the maelstrom.

Freddie scampered around the field, while some of the boys continued to play ball—and others chased after the delighted dog. Freddie wove in and out and around the players with surprising adroitness, a canine agility champ in the making, spraying mud and wet clumps of grass as he went. He showed no interest whatsoever in the ball, but rather enjoyed this mad scrambling game of tag, in which he was definitely *it*.

There were shouts and jeers and finally, the shrill whistle of the referee. Everyone on the field froze in place; even Freddie stopped short for a minute, panting, his lips drawn back, his pink tongue hanging out. But then he rocketed down the field again.

I was frozen, too. I stood with Shakespeare's leash in my hand, rooted to the sidelines, and watched the cavorting canine with a frustration that dissolved into tears.

"Get that animal off the field!" The ref looked at me, a sopping wet, sobbing, single mom who couldn't control her dog or her boyfriend or her life. "Is that mutt yours?"

"He's not a mutt," I said. "He's a beagle. Purebred."

"I don't care if he's the champ of Westminster. Get him out of here."

"The leash broke." I threw up my hands. "I'm so sorry, I—"

The ref interrupted me with another sharp shriek of his whistle.

The boys had cornered Freddie at the end of the field, down by the goalposts. Mikey was the goalie. He held his arms outstretched in front of him, trying to keep the dog confined to the net. Freddie thought it was a game, and kept biting Mikey's gloves.

"Put your hands down, Mikey, and he'll come to you," I said.

Mikey dropped his arms to his sides and slumped to his knees. "Freddie!" he called. "Come here, boy!"

The unapologetic beagle trotted over to Mikey and licked his nose. As the boys cheered and laughed, Mikey hugged him to his chest. Then he stood up and handed the slimy little creature over to me. "Don't drop him, Mom."

I held Freddie like a baby, on my left close to my heart, and trudged back to the car, Shakespeare on my heels. I deposited the soggy, sorry lump of puppy meat on the back seat. Shakespeare hopped in next to Freddie. I slammed the door shut, then opened the rear hatch of the mini-SUV and threw the beach chair in on top of the snow brushes and salt bags and jumper cables. I slammed that door shut, too, and then plopped into the driver's seat. I planned to sit out the rest of the game safely in my Kia, heat on high and windshield wipers slapping the spitting rain away so I could watch my son's team lose yet another game in relative comfort. If I concentrated hard enough, I'd be able to ignore the dusky, malodorous wet dog smell that now perfumed my personal space.

Mikey's team was new, formed by the leftovers of other, more-established teams. Mikey had played goalie on a winning team back in Salem, so playing on this inept lineup was a real comedown for him. Worse, he blamed himself every time they lost a game.

"I'm the goalie, Mom," he told me after another humiliating defeat. "I'm supposed to stop the other team from scoring."

"You are not the reason your team keeps losing, honey." Raising two boys had taught me a sports cliché or two. I knew the ins and outs of winning and losing. "You can't win playing defense. It takes a good offense. You need to score to win. Your team never scores."

"We're pathetic. I'm quitting."

We'd been through this before. "No, you're not. You made a commitment to the team, and you will honor that commitment." This was one of the few Colonel's Rules of Life I actually managed to follow and instill in my children as well. Not that Mikey much liked it. But he stayed on the team.

Mercifully, the rain let up. That, coupled with the Freddie interlude, seemed to recharge Mikey's team. Their spirits rose, and their playing improved. Mikey redoubled his efforts, too. As goalie, he kept the other team at bay—which in all honesty was not particularly difficult, as their opponents never got near the goal with the ball.

Miraculously, Mikey's pal Jacob scored a goal—the first and only goal of the game. Mikey's team won—their first and only win of the season.

All of the parents poured out of their vehicles to congratulate their sons on this once-in-a-season victory. Me, too—but I left the dogs in the car. Mikey ran up to me, grinning.

"We won, Mom! We really won!"

"That's great, honey!" I gave him a quick hug.

"They didn't score a single goal against me."

"No, they didn't. You did a great job, just like you always do." I pushed the damp curls clamped to his brow by the rain out of his shining face. "But that's not why you didn't lose like all the other times. This time, your offense actually scored. And—"

"You have to score to win." Mikey finished my lecture for me. "I get it, Mom."

I smiled. "Good."

Mikey clambered into the front passenger seat. "The coach is taking us all out for pizza to celebrate. Can you drop me off at the Center?"

"Sure." Maybe all this socializing with the soccer team meant more new friends for Mikey. I thanked God for the coach, for the win, and the sport of soccer as we drove away from the field.

Freddie rushed forward, and Mikey let the little pooch push his way onto his buddy's lap. "I think Freddie's the reason we won that game, Mom. He's our lucky charm."

"Maybe." I laughed. "Shall I arrange for Freddie to break his leash and take to the field every game?"

Mikey laughed, too. "That's okay. There are only a few more games and then the season's over." He gave me a stern look. "And then I'm done with soccer. Seriously."

"We'll talk about it later—"

"Mom, I'm twelve years old." Mikey paused dramatically. "I can no longer be seen in public in these soccer shorts."

I bit my lip hard to keep from laughing, and averted my eyes, keeping them peeled to the road ahead of me. Within minutes, Mikey and Freddie were asleep. All that rain and ruckus had worn them out. By the time we pulled into the small, outdated strip mall known to locals as the Center, it was getting dark. There was a liquor store, a candy shop, and a pizzeria, anchored by a CVS pharmacy and Rocky's Ace Hardware. They were always talking about tearing it down and building a Super Stop and Shop, but it never happened.

"Mikey, we're here." I shook my tired son gently by the shoulder.

"Okay, Mom, I'm going."

I held Freddie tightly by his collar while Mikey jumped out.

He gave Freddie a final pat. "Thanks, Freddie. Thanks for helping us win."

I waved goodbye to my son, watched him as he disappeared into the pizza parlor, and then drove on home with the dogs. I had a lot to do to prepare for the party tomorrow, the housewarming celebration that Mikey and I would host alone.

Later that evening, I tucked a happy if weary boy and his happy if weary beagle into bed. I turned on the stove, and prepared my award-winning chili for the next day, drinking wine and listening to Patsy

Cline croon "Crazy" and reminding myself that Dorothy Parker drank herself to death and James Thurber was an alcoholic misogynist of the first order who liked dogs better than women.

If turnaround is fair play, well, then I liked dogs better than Thurber.

chapter seven

"Each dog is an individual possessing possibilities that may truly surprise us."

—THE MONKS OF NEW SKETE

T HE DAY OF THE PARTY DAWNED CLEAR AND PURE AND BRIGHT, A perfect Indian summer day that shimmered in sun and light and color. Yesterday's rain had scrubbed the air, leaving behind only the faint scent of green. It was the kind of day that casts an optimistic glow, and I was prepared to bask in it.

The cottage shone with promise, clean and neat and full of freshly cut sunflowers I'd bought at the farm stand down the road. The dogs were clean, too, thanks to the obligatory baths I'd given the muddy mutts after the soccer game. I used my own conditioner on Shakespeare's thick mane, and his black spiky fur was soft and silky to the touch. Freddie's fur gleamed thanks to my lavender shampoo and once again he sported that sweet-and-sour puppy smell that could render even the most sensible humans senseless. Thurber was gone, but it didn't matter. Part of me was ashamed that I had no official host for my open house—and part of me was ashamed that I felt that way. I'd told Joel that Thurber wasn't coming, after all, hoping he would step in as the host. But

Joel wasn't big on parties, no matter who was in attendance. I knew
he wouldn't come. Which was just as well.

This was our home, Mikey's and mine. It was just the two of us—
and Isis and Shakespeare and now Freddie. Mikey was thrilled that
Thurber was gone, and excited about the party, so excited that when
I wasn't looking he took a can of bright blue spray paint and painted
the side of the concrete retaining wall that flanked the septic mound
to read: *Paula and Mikey Live Here.* Just in case there was any
doubt on the part of the thirty-plus people who showed up at our cottage on the lake that glorious autumn afternoon.

They came from all over—old friends from Salem, former colleagues from Rockport, new neighbors from the lake, current colleagues from Avon, Thurber's cousins from southern Vermont.

Thurber's cousins from southern Vermont. Maybe Thurber
had decided to skip the housewarming party, but apparently his family had not.

"We know Thurber isn't here, but we came anyway," Thurber's
affable cousin George said by way of explanation when he and his
wife showed up at my front door, bearing gifts of wine and cheese
and spinach dip.

"We like you," chimed in Gloria, George's adorable wife.

"I like you, too," I said. And I did. Thurber's cousins were wonderful people, kind and loving and generous. I'd spent more than one
enjoyable holiday dinner at their inviting home up North. "I'm glad
you came."

All the other guests at the open house found it challenging, trying
to remember not to bash Thurber while his cousins were in the same
room. But after enough drinking margaritas and eating my award-
winning chili and basking in the late afternoon sun, nobody cared any
more. Everyone loved everybody else, no matter whom they were
related to.

Despite my embarrassment it was clear that I didn't need a host.
I had Mikey, the little man of the house. And Mikey had Freddie, who

charmed them all. The cheerful beagle trotted from guest to guest, wooing each with those pretty Bette Davis eyes in turn. He sniffed and licked and wagged and whimpered and pushed his wet nose anywhere he thought it might benefit him to do so. And it benefited him enormously.

My boss's daughter, a hyper-intelligent five-year-old named Hannah, adopted Freddie at first lick.

"What can he do?" Hannah asked Mikey.

Mikey regarded Hannah with the distant bemusement with which he regarded all little girls. "What do you mean?"

"Can he sit, stay, shake?" Hannah took a deep breath and continued. "Roll over, play dead, fetch, catch a Frisbee, high-five, beg, take a bow?"

"Take a bow?" Mikey shook his head, laughing. "No, but he can take a p—"

"Mikey!" I interrupted him just in time, pulling him aside. "She's five, Mikey."

"She's awful bossy for five," Mikey said.

"I heard that," Hannah said.

"She's a big sister," I whispered. "All big sisters are bossy."

"She's not *my* big sister."

"I'm not bossy," Hannah said, tossing her ponytail for emphasis. "But you should be training him. He's a puppy. Puppies need training."

"Go ahead," Mikey said, handing Freddie's leash to the little girl. "Knock yourself out. I gotta fire up the Weber."

So while Mikey flipped burgers on the Weber for the growing crowd, Hannah took it upon herself to train Freddie to sit. She dogged the recalcitrant puppy's every step, monitored his every move, directed his every, well, direction. By the end of the afternoon, when Hannah said, "Sit!" Freddie sat.

Hannah was very pleased with herself. She pulled Freddie by his lead all over the yard, up and down the deck, all round the house, showing everyone how she'd taught Freddie to sit in only one day.

"I just love it," I told my friend Wendy as we stood in the kitchen drinking wine and bashing men and dogs and publishers. We'd worked together at Rockport. "In the two months we've had him, we haven't been able to teach that puppy a thing. But one little five-year-old girl Freddie's never even met before teaches him one of the major commands in minutes."

Wendy laughed. "Well, *she* means business—and Freddie knows it." Wendy poured us each another glass of wine, and I knew I was in for it. "They're really nice," she said, tossing her head in the direction of Thurber's cousins.

"Yes, they are."

"I can't believe they came anyway."

I smiled. "They're *really* nice."

Wendy sipped her wine. "Has he called you yet?"

I sipped some wine of my own. "Not yet."

"I'm surprised." Wendy checked the big French clock that hung over the kitchen table. "It's been twenty-four hours already. He's running late."

"He won't call. Not this time."

Wendy pursed her lips. "He *will* call, you know."

"I don't think so. That woman—"

"He always calls wanting to come back. It's just a matter of time."

I gulped down the rest of my wine. "Doesn't matter either way."

"You're done?" Wendy looked at me. "You're really done?"

I nodded.

"You have to show him you mean business, then. Just like Hannah did with Freddie."

"*Yeah.* Men are dogs, may as well train them the same way." I giggled. Grown women should never giggle. No more wine for me.

"Just don't answer."

I giggled again. "What?"

"When he calls." Wendy looked at me sternly. "Just don't answer."

"I won't," I promised. "I'm done with him."

Thurber started calling around six o'clock, not long after the last guest left the lake. I was standing on the dock in the growing darkness, watching the stars appear in the sky, trying not to cry. Mikey was inside the house playing video games; I was on dog duty. Shakespeare stood beside me, alert to my tears; Freddie pulled on his leash, lunging at the ducks that swam too close to shore, oblivious to my pain. Just like Thurber.

"Sit!" I said, trying to mean business, just the way Hannah did.

Freddie did not sit. Apparently I did not mean business.

When I was a little girl, I saw a movie with my mother called *If a Man Answers*. Sandra Dee played a newlywed whose Parisian mother gives her a dog-training book and instructs her to apply the same guiding principles to her husband (played by Bobby Darin) as she does to her poodle. To the young wife's surprise, it works—and before long her husband comes when she calls him, hankers to go on long walks with her, and always begs for treats.

My mother loved that movie. I always thought it was because she loved all Sixties-era romantic comedies, beginning and ending with Doris Day and Rock Hudson. But now I believed that she was trying to teach me something about the relationship between men and women—and the lengths to which we women must go to train our men to be good husbands. My mother had this instruction down; she could have been a drill sergeant in a former life.

The lessons of Sandra Dee and Bobby Darin were wasted on me. I failed to train Freddie; I failed to train Thurber. They didn't come when I called, they wandered away from me on long walks, and the only person begging was me. Apparently it was far easier to train poodles and Frenchmen than beagles and Bostonians.

I'd like to tell you that I didn't answer when he called, but you know I'd just be lying.

chapter eight

"Adolescent Beagles can be particularly stubborn creatures."

—KRISTINE KRAEUTER, *Training Your Beagle*

THURBER ASIDE, THE HOUSEWARMING PARTY PROVED A RESOUNDING success—and testimony to the fact that this move had been the right one, after all. Life at our little lakeside house in Lytton was taking shape. We took the paddle boat out on the water; Mikey mastered the art of catching, filleting, and frying up the lake's bass; we shared fish suppers on the back porch and watched the geese flying south over the great pond.

Mikey didn't have a best friend in the seventh grade yet—Louie down the street was his pal but did not really qualify as a best friend—but he did have one at home: Freddie. The spirited little dog followed Mikey wherever he went, curled up on the boy's lap while he watched TV, and slept head to head with him on matching down-filled pillows every night while the dog crate sat empty at the foot of the bed. So much for crate training.

In short, I was feeling very pleased with myself. True, I'd suffered a relapse or two in regard to Thurber, but no permanent damage was done. I was focused now solely on my son and our new life on the South Shore. And it was paying off.

Self-congratulation always invited disaster—and mine was no exception. I was at work when I got the call.

"Your son Michael has been suspended from school. I'm afraid you'll have to come down to the office and pick him up immediately," said the vice principal at Lytton Middle School.

"Suspended?" I was stunned. Unlike his older brother, Greg, who'd been suspended from school every year from the third grade on, Mikey had never gotten into trouble like this before. Mikey didn't talk back to teachers or vandalize school property or skip class or make out with girls in the gym or smoke cigarettes in the boys' bathroom—at least he hadn't so far. All of which Greg had done by junior high. The thought that Mikey could be pulling a Greg—and that this could be the first in a long series of Greg-style incidents—terrified me. I just didn't know if I could go through all that again. "What did he do?"

"We'd prefer to discuss the incident in person," the vice principal said.

Great, I thought on my hour drive to the middle school. All I needed was another juvenile delinquent on my hands. I'd survived Greg's adolescence—just barely—but I didn't have to face it alone. I was married and living down the road from my folks. This time I'd have no backup: I had no husband and the Colonel was thousands of miles away in Las Vegas.

Mikey was sitting in the school office on a plastic chair, his backpack at his feet. He looked at me and shrugged. The school secretary ushered me past my son into the vice principal's office and then retreated, shutting the door behind her.

Mr. Carrington, as the kids called him, walked around his desk to greet me. He shook my hand. "Have a seat."

I sat down, straight-backed, prepared to fight for my child. School authorities always brought out the warrior in me; the same bureaucratic sensibility that I railed against at the RMV reigned at schools—and I would not acquiesce without a fight. When Mikey's first-grade teacher in Las Vegas enlisted an entire boardroom full of educational experts—from the principal to the school counselor—to try to convince me that my six-year-old needed Ritalin, I stared them all down, belittled her teaching methods and classroom managements skills, and produced an exam from Mikey's physician that proved he did not have the attention deficit disorder or learning disabilities she claimed that he had. In fact, he started first grade already reading at a third-grade level. I found out later that Mikey wasn't the only boy in her class she wanted to medicate into submission. She'd tried to convince all the mothers of the male children in her class that they needed "help." In the end, they left Mikey alone, and shortly thereafter I moved with Mikey to Massachusetts, where the very first day his new teacher walked Mikey out to the car to tell me that my son was "wicked smart."

Massachusetts has great public schools; the state consistently ranks at the top nationwide in public education. More kids go on to college in Massachusetts than in any other state in the union. When we were looking for a house on the South Shore, we focused our attention on Lytton because of its commitment to its schools.

But that didn't mean I trusted them.

The vice principal handed me a note scribbled on lined paper. In very sloppy handwriting I recognized as Mikey's, the note read in French: *Donnez-moi l'argent ou je vais vous terminer.* Translation: Give me the money or I'll terminate you.

"Michael has physically threatened the French teacher," Mr. Carrington said. "We have a zero-tolerance policy when it comes to violence."

"Violence?" I stared at Mr. Carrington. "That's ridiculous. Mikey isn't violent."

Mr. Carrington went on. "He's suspended for a week—and he can't come back to school until you have a psychologist's report saying he's not a threat to himself or others."

"Impossible," I said. "He would never do that—threaten anybody. It must be some sort of misunderstanding."

"We're investigating," the vice principal said. "Talking to all the people involved. In the meantime, you have to take Michael home."

"I'll be doing some investigating of my own." I pulled myself up to my full height and regarded Mr. Carrington sternly. "I know what it means to mark a kid this way. I won't let you get away with it." I strode out of Mr. Carrington's office, tossed my head at Mikey, and marched my son down the hall and out of the building. Neither of us said a word until we got into the car.

"Mom—"

"Let's wait until we get home," I said. "We need to talk face to face."

Once we got home, Mikey curled up on the couch with Freddie on his lap. I sat down on the ottoman across from them.

"Talk to me," I said.

"It's not fair," Mikey said, burying his face in Freddie's fur. "It was just part of the play."

"Play? Did you say play?" I reached over and placed my hand under his chin and lifted it gently. "You need to sit up, honey. I can't understand you when you're mumbling into Freddie's neck."

Mikey sighed. "It was an assignment. Write a little scene in French and act it out. We didn't want to do anything stupid like being American tourists asking 'where is the train station?'" He looked up at me, defiant. "That's just lame."

"I see," I said. "So what did you do?"

"I thought it would be cool if our group did a bank robbery."

"A bank robbery," I repeated.

"Yeah. You know, a robber comes into the bank and gives a note to the teller—"

"Oh my God," I said, putting two and two together.

"I was just writing down what the robber's note would say, Mom." Mikey shook his head. "I didn't mean—"

"What did the note say?" I wanted to hear him say it.

"It said: *Donnez-moi l'argent ou je vais vous terminer.*" Mikey grinned in spite of himself.

"*Give me the money or* . . . ." I faltered.

"*I'll terminate you*," Mikey finished for me. "I was just taking notes for the play, Mom. But I left the paper at my desk by accident and after class was over and I was gone the teacher found it and freaked out."

"And you wrote it *in French*?"

"It was a writing assignment, Mom. For French class." Mikey threw up his hands. "I swear, Mom. Ask any of the kids in my class."

"I will." I pointed my finger at him. "That said, criminal activity is not an appropriate subject for school assignments," I told him harshly. "No more video games for you. For a month."

"Give me a break." Mikey rolled his eyes. "You write about murder all the time, Mom."

He had me there. I loved everything about murder mysteries—reading them, watching them, and writing them. An active member of the Mystery Writers of America, I was halfway through my first thriller, which featured three murders as presently outlined, maybe more by the time I was finished with the manuscript. My writer's group, known as the Monday Murder Club, met at the cottage every Monday night, where we read our work in progress aloud—a merry mortal mix of shootings, stabbings, and serial killings.

Not that we restricted murder to Mondays. On most every other night of the week as well, Mikey and I watched murder and mayhem together: *CSI*, *Monk*, the aforementioned *Numb3rs*, PBS's *Mystery!* (which was my very favorite show of all time, not that Mikey much liked it).

"I'm not in the seventh grade," I said. "I'm not in school."

"I get it, Mom. I'll never do anything like that again." He turned to Freddie for comfort, scratching his puppy's ears and letting the little beagle lick his chin in return. "But come on, Mom. I wasn't threatening the teacher. How could anyone believe that?" He looked at me, and said in a small voice, "You don't believe that, do you, Mom?"

"No, actually I don't." I patted his hand. "And I'm going to do what I can. But schools have rules. And we have to follow them. *You* have to follow them."

"Okay, Mom." He gave me a hug. "I love you."

"I love you, too, sweetie."

I talked to all of Mikey's friends, including the ones in his French class, and some grownups, too. As it turned out, Mikey wasn't the only student who'd had trouble in this teacher's class. In fact, several parents had pulled their kids out of the class and switched them to woodworking or independent study or choir. I also researched therapists; within a couple of days I found Dr. Santori, a dapper Italian psychologist who radiated intelligence and calm.

Mikey and I went to see him the next day. I sat in the waiting room reading an old copy of *Ladies Home Journal* while Mikey and Dr. Santori talked about God knows what. I knew from my divorces that counselors worked with kids in mysterious ways. All of my children had gone to counselors in the wake of my broken marriages—and they all learned from it. If only I had as well. I must be doing something wrong since I was spending so much time in therapists' waiting rooms while my children worked through problems that one way or another were the painful result of my mistakes.

After a fifty-minute session with Mikey, Dr. Santori called me into his office. He agreed that Mikey was not a danger to himself or to others, and he filled out the forms that the school needed for Mikey to return.

"I'm going right to the vice principal with these forms," I told Dr. Santori. "I'm going to insist that they fire that woman. Or at least move Mikey to another class."

"I think it's perfectly reasonable to request a classroom change," Dr. Santori said.

"Great." I got up to go, extending my hand. "Thanks so much for all your help. We really appreciate it, especially on such short notice."

"I'm afraid we're not quite finished." Dr. Santori motioned me back to my seat with a wave of his hand.

I sank into the plump chair. "What's wrong?"

"I think Michael would benefit from continued therapy," Dr. Santori said. "He seems to have some issues around the divorce to work out. His father, his stepmother, you . . . ." His voice trailed off.

"I thought he had worked through most of that." I hesitated. "You know, after the divorce. I hoped that leaving California, moving here . . . ." My voice trailed off.

"But Michael does visit his father frequently," Dr. Santori said.

"Yes," I conceded. "He does. But his real life is here."

Dr. Santori smiled. "It's all Michael's real life—there and here."

"I know." I looked down at my hands in my lap.

"Michael's on the brink of adolescence now," said Dr. Santori. "Adolescence brings up all kinds of new concerns and preoccupations."

"Don't I know it."

"Why do you say that?"

"I know from my older son Greg," I explained. "His teenage years were rough on all of us. He was very rebellious." I lifted my head and looked Dr. Santori in the eye. "Whatever we have to do to avoid going through that, we'll do."

Mikey didn't say anything on our ride back home. He stared out the car window, his jaw tight.

"Mikey, it's not forever—"

"You said you believed me," he said just loud enough for me to hear him. "It wasn't my fault."

"I did believe you, I *do* believe you," I said. "And I'm telling the vice principal that tomorrow."

"There's nothing wrong with me."

"You're right," I said. "There's nothing wrong with you. I know that. Dr. Santori knows that, too. But you need someone to talk to. Besides me. About your father, your stepmother, even me."

"I have nothing to say."

"We both know that's not true, honey."

When we got home, we found Freddie in the kitchen with Shakespeare, right where we'd left him. But he'd chewed all the wooden knobs off my custom cherry cabinets. The gnawed-off remains of the round pulls were scattered across the floor. Freddie cocked his head, tail wagging, big brown eyes proclaiming his innocence even as the wood slivers in his mouth confirmed his guilt.

"Freddie!" I didn't know whether to kill him—or kill him.

"Don't yell at him, Mom. He's just a puppy."

"He's not a puppy any more, Mikey, he's nearly a year old." I threw my purse on the table and grabbed Freddie's leash. "He needs to learn some manners. You need to teach him some manners." I snapped the lead on the wayward mutt's collar and called for Shakespeare. "I'm taking them out. You clean up this mess."

I walked through the house to the back porch and directed Freddie and Shakespeare over to the side yard. While they sniffed around for the best places to leave their mark, I looked out over the lake at the long, V-shaped string of ducks flying south for the winter. The crack of a rifle echoed across the water, and a bird fell from the sky. I turned toward the island, where the hunters lie in wait. I felt like the fowl, hounded by a change in season. Winter could be a dangerous time.

If only Freddie and Mikey could be all grown up by spring. But as I knew all too well from past experience, adolescence was a virus that lasted at least five years in human boys. I wondered how long it lasted in beagles.

chapter nine

"Given the relative scarcity of barking in wolves, some theorize that dogs have developed a more elaborate barking language precisely in order to communicate with humans."

—ALEXANDRA HOROWITZ, *Inside of a Dog*

I TALKED TO MR. CARRINGTON, THE VICE PRINCIPAL AT LYTTON MIDDLE School, and Mikey left the French class. Mikey continued to see Dr. Santori, and whatever they talked about Mikey mostly kept to himself. When I did sit in, it was mostly to discuss grades (he didn't care enough about them to do his homework), and girls (he cared enough about them to douse himself with Axe cologne every morning before going to school), and going to see his father (he cared, he didn't care, depending on the day and/or his mood).

Meanwhile, Freddie talked to everyone and everything—me, Mikey, Isis, Shakespeare, neighbors, friends, visitors, other dogs, other cats, birds, squirrels, the wind in the trees, the boats on the lake, the cars on the road, UPS drivers at the front door, pizza deliverymen at the front door, Jehovah's Witnesses at the front door, everyone at the front door. Freddie found his voice—and it was an arf, a bark, a bawl, a bay, a bellow, a bow-wow, a cry, a growl, a groan, a grunt, a moan, a roar, a ruff, a pant, a scream, a snarl, a snuffle, a squeal, a wail, a whine, a whimper, a woof, a yip, a yap, a yelp, a yowl—and, ultimately, a howl.

All this conversation—if you deign to call it conversation—was contagious. Shakespeare, who never in the more than six years we'd had him had ever been much of a barker, now chimed in on every communication. It was the dueling banjos of barking. Anything Freddie could do, Shakespeare felt honor-bound to do better—one decibel at a time.

Isis didn't care for all this commotion, and added her complaining mews and meows and shrieks and screeches to the din. Mikey yelled at the dogs, I yelled at Mikey, and what it all added up to was a heck of a lot of noise.

The neighbors started to complain. Steve, the good-natured pharmaceutical salesman next door with whom we shared a fence and a property line, couldn't walk outside of his own house without Freddie and Shakespeare going crazy, releasing a cacophony of barking. All of us on the lake spent a lot of time outside, hanging out on our respective docks, doing yard work, fishing and boating and swimming—and Steve was no exception. Steve had a jet ski and a boat and water trampoline; all the kids in the neighborhood—including Mikey—loved him. Steve liked us, but he hated Freddie. He dropped by with a couple of computer printouts.

"Look," Steve said. "I found these special collars on the Internet. They're guaranteed to stop barking."

"I don't know." I studied the printouts. "These are shock collars."

"One does provide a slight electrical shock," Steve conceded, "but the other one just sprays the dog with citronella when he barks."

"I see."

"It's better than taking out his voice box," Steve said. "I had friends who had to do that to their dog. Weird—not to mention expensive."

"Let me see what I can do about that," I promised.

And I did. I blew fifty bucks on one of those spray collars and tried it on Freddie. Freddie didn't mind the spray so much; he just licked the water around his chops. He certainly didn't find it uncomfortable enough to affect his marathon barking. Eventually, Freddie ate it, as he'd eaten countless collars before.

Winter came early that year. By early November there was already snow on the ground, and the lake was beginning to freeze over. Saturday morning Mikey took the dogs out and tied them up to the long runners in the side yard. He came back inside and settled in the living room in front of the TV to play his new video game. I was in the shower. Even standing under all that running water I could hear Freddie howling, but I didn't pay much attention; after all, Freddie was always howling. He was nothing if not a vocal dog.

But the little dog with the big mouth was still baying when I got out of the shower. I got dressed quickly and went to the kitchen to start breakfast.

"Pancakes or bacon and eggs?" I asked Mikey.

"Bacon and eggs."

"Okay, well, while I fry up the bacon, you go get that dog. You know the Barking Rule." The barking rule was this: Don't let the dogs bark outside for more than fifteen minutes—or else the neighbors were bound to complain. We'd timed it over the past several weeks and we knew that the most complaints came after twenty minutes of nonstop howling. Apparently that was the point at which the average human felt driven to silence the average beagle, even if it meant getting up off the couch and walking down the road and over to our house to complain. So we short-circuited this neighborly impulse by bringing the dogs inside after fifteen minutes.

"Mom, I'm busy."

"No dogs, no eggs."

Mikey grudgingly paused his computer game on the one and only television in our cottage. "Don't go changing the channel to HGTV." He pulled himself heavily to his feet, pulled the hood of his sweatshirt up over his ears, and trudged outside to retrieve Freddie and

Shakespeare—but five minutes later Shakespeare was the only dog to accompany my son back into the house.

"Freddie's gone, Mom," said Mikey all in a rush.

"But I can still *hear* him."

"He's gone, Mom! Come on!"

I slipped on a sweater and ran out the back door through the porch to the landing above the dock, Mikey and Shakespeare right behind me.

My hand shielding the bright sun that glinted on the icy surface of the lake, I peered in the direction of the baying beagle. I didn't see anything at first—and then the sun slipped behind a cloud and *bingo!* there was Freddie, out in the middle of the half-frozen lake, howling his little silky-eared head off.

"Mom, the ice is cracking all around him! He's going to drown!"

"He's not going to drown." I pointed out across the lake at the distressed hound. "He got out there somehow on solid ice, all he has to do is come back the way he came."

"He's too scared, Mom. He's too scared to move." Mikey headed for the dock. "I'm gonna go get him."

"No, you aren't." I grabbed the hood of his sweatshirt and pulled him back to me. "You're a lot heavier than that dog. You'll break the ice for sure and sink like a stone."

"What are we going to do?"

"We just need to coax him home."

Steve appeared in the yard, along with a couple of other neighbors from farther down the road. They all lived on the lake.

"We've been trying to call him in off the ice," Steve said. "But he won't come for us."

"Why don't you come down to the long dock," Harold said. Harold had three Weimaraners, none of whom were stuck out on the frozen lake squealing like a pig. "That way you can get closer to him."

"Good idea," I said. Our short dock didn't extend more than ten feet into the lake, if that. But there were far longer docks on our side of the lake.

We all sprinted down around the curve in the road where one of our fellow residents had an extensive dock that ran some forty feet into the lake. On the way, we passed Edna, the retired elderly lady with the black cat, standing outside on her postage-stamp front porch looking worried.

"I called the police," Edna told me, "to come and rescue the poor little guy."

Lord, I thought, not again. My house was becoming the go-to place in town for cops.

"Um, thanks," I said. "But I do hope that won't be necessary."

We walked on to Mary's house, an adorable, neatly maintained two-story shingled cottage with a prettily designed garden to match. It was the one place I most hoped that my cottage would someday resemble. We went around Mary's home to the lakeside, where a narrow pier stretched out deep into the lake. A perfectly placed Adirondack chair anchored its end point.

I strode out on the planked dock, all the way to the water's edge. Freddie sat on his haunches in the middle of the partially frozen pond, head back, long ears lank against his neck, nose to the open sky, mouth a howling drawl that ricocheted around the lake.

"Freddie!" I yelled.

Freddie stopped mid-howl, and craned his neck in my general direction. He regarded me with what appeared to be alarm, rather than relief.

"Freddie!" I yelled, louder this time, and his cursed moniker echoed across the ice. *Freddie! Freddie! Freddie!*

All those "Freddie!s" provoked the frightened hound into a noisy return volley of bays and bawls.

This was not working. Freddie was not responding to me. The cops were on their way. What to do? I fought a raging impulse to charge across the ice and pull the blasted little beagle home by his tail. But I knew that was not a good option, even had I not been wearing my new knee-high riding boots. I needed a more subtle approach.

On my tenth birthday the Colonel surprised me with an eight-week-old black poodle puppy. We were stationed in Germany at the time, living outside of Mainz in a small compound in Gonsenheim in officer's quarters built by the French after the First World War. If you're German and you have a dog—and you'd be hard-pressed to find a German without one—odds are you have a German shepherd, a dachshund, or a French poodle. Which as any German will be happy to inform you, is a misnomer. French poodles aren't French at all. Let the French call the poodle the national dog of France if they will; Germans know they're really German dogs, water retrievers and truffle hunters who take their name from the German *pudel* or *pudelin*, which means "to splash in the water."

Just for the record: there is nothing on earth cuter than the lively ball of fluff that is a poodle puppy. Of course, a poodle was not exactly my father's kind of dog; no self-respecting male—much less a soldier!—would be seen in the company of such a girly dog. But I was a girl, so he got me what he thought of as a girl's dog. He was no doubt influenced by our neighbors, the Landers, who lived across the hall.

The Landers had three daughters—Harriet, Henrietta, and Linda—and three poodles—Pierre, Monique, and Zsa Zsa. These dogs were smart, sassy, sophisticated creatures who could perform any number of tricks—from fetching balls and walking on their hind legs to sipping champagne and enchanting all who encountered them. Perfectly groomed and well-mannered, they were the Audrey Hepburn, Cary Grant, and Grace Kelly of dogs. Even my mother liked them—and she didn't care for dogs. And my father, whose taste in canines ran to more manly breeds such as Weimaraners and vizslas and Great Danes, admitted with a grudging admiration that the Landers's poodles were "damned smart dogs."

And so I got a poodle, as smart a girly dog as my dad could find. I was enchanted with Rogue, as we christened him at my mother's suggestion after much debate over what to name the very best birthday present I'd ever gotten in my short life. I spent every waking minute outside of the legally mandated school hours with my new best friend. When he wasn't with me, Rogue was with my mother, who for the first time in her life actually enjoyed having a dog in the house. We both babied him, cooing and caressing and cuddling. We bathed him and combed his thick curly coat and tied ribbons to his topknot and tail and called him by such diminutives as "Rogue-y" and "Rogue-y-poo."

Socialization was no problem for Rogue; we had a neighborhood full of dogs and kids and we played with them all. Not to mention that the clever puppy befriended his fellow poodles across the hall—and they taught him everything they knew within weeks.

Rogue was nearly a year old when Mom and I went on a Girl Scout trip to Switzerland, leaving the Colonel in charge of Rogue. Dad and dogs went together like guns and roses, so we didn't worry about them while we were touring the International Girl Scouts Chalet high in the Alps in Adelboden. But when we got home, the Landers couldn't wait to tell us about the Colonel and the poodle.

"Your father let Rogue out every night," Mrs. Landers said to me, eyes bright with contained laughter, "just like you do. Only when you take him out, he always comes back when you call him."

My mother and I stared at Mrs. Landers. Mr. Landers started to laugh. Dad shook his head.

"Are you saying that when Paul called Rogue to come, he didn't come?" my mother asked.

Mr. Landers laughed harder.

"Goddamn dog," my father said.

"No, he wouldn't come when your father called him," Mrs. Landers said. "At least not at first."

"But Rogue always comes when you call him," I said.

"All dogs come when the Colonel calls them," my mother added. "Remember Red? Tell them about Red, Paul."

My father started to laugh, too.

I didn't see what was so funny about Rogue not doing what the Colonel told him to do. Good puppies were supposed to follow orders, just like good soldiers. Just like the rest of us.

"Not Rogue," my dad said.

"Not Rogue," Mrs. Landers repeated. "Your father called and called for him, but he didn't come, until . . . ." She paused dramatically. "Until he called for him like you do."

"Like I do," I said, confused. "What do you mean?"

"Rogue-y!" sang my father in a high falsetto. "Rogue-y-poo!" The Colonel did a dead-on imitation of my high-pitched ten-year-old pre-pubescent girl's cadence.

At the sound of "my" voice, Rogue came running. The Colonel shrugged. My mother laughed until she cried.

If it worked for the Colonel, maybe it would work for me. I called for Freddie again, this time in the same sharp lilt I'd used as a child to call my beloved Rogue.

"Freeeeeddddieee!" I crooned. "Freddie-poo!"

The howl died in Freddie's mouth. He cocked his head, listening.

"Come here, baby! Come here!"

Freddie scrambled to his feet, tail wagging. He bounded forward, slipping and sliding on his paws across the ice. Scared, he skidded to a stop, still several hundred yards from the dock.

"Good boy, Freddie!" I sounded like an out-of-work extra from a Gilbert and Sullivan operetta. But it worked.

Slowly but surely, to the lullaby tune of my high-pitched pleading, Freddie picked his way across the icy pond. By the time he made it to the dock where I stood waiting for him, Freddie was shivering from the cold, I was hoarse, and the neighbors were applauding.

I leaned over to lift the pathetic half-frozen pooch off the ice and into my arms. I cuddled him close to my chest and carried him home like the baby he was, Mikey hot on our heels.

Mikey took Freddie into the bathroom to rub the frigid puppy down with my good Egyptian towels, and I called the local police and told them not to bother coming out, that Freddie Munier, the wayward hound, had been rescued from certain death.

"We could hear him howling all the way down here at the station," the dispatcher said. "We got lots of calls about it."

"I'm so sorry," I said and hung up. The Colonel would have been proud.

Not long afterwards my friend Charlie came to visit. Charlie was my real-estate advisor, the financier who'd convinced me that I could afford my own home in the first place. He saw me through the housing search process and helped me arrange the loan for the house. He inspected all the places in which I'd shown a real interest—and steered me clear of the ones he thought would prove to be a poor investment.

Charlie was a very tall, dashing Irish Catholic Bostonian who was as comfortable shooting a moose as he was analyzing a spreadsheet. When he went hunting, he flew his pack of hunting dogs with him in a chartered jet to such hunting meccas as Wyoming and Montana. He knew from hunting dogs.

Freddie and Shakespeare were tied up on their runners on the septic mound side yard when Charlie pulled up in his Ford Explorer for his biannual visit. Freddie began his usual manic barking and Shakespeare joined in. I came out onto the front deck to greet Charlie and shush the dogs—not that they paid any attention.

"Are these noisy guys yours?" Charlie asked, laughing at the din.

"Yes." I ran down to intercept him. "You might want to wait until I calm Freddie down. I'm trying to teach him not to bark so much. And sometimes he lunges—"

"Little chance of that." Charlie was already loping up the septic mound to where the dogs pulled at their runners, Freddie baying wildly at the imposing six-feet-seven interloper who loomed over them, while Shakespeare silently sized up the man. Charlie dropped to a squat and the dogs lunged. He just chuckled and opened his palms. Freddie and Shakespeare licked his fingers, and Charlie scratched their ears.

"Nice dogs," Charlie told me. "Shall I bring them inside?"

"Sure." Obviously Charlie knew what he was doing. He unhooked the dogs from their runners and they happily followed the Piped Piper of Hunting Dogs into the cottage. We settled on the couch in front of the fireplace, and Freddie curled up at Charlie's feet.

"He likes you."

Charlie looked at me, a look that would have undone any other woman. He was the kind of man women went weak at the knees for— so tall, so handsome, so rich. My friend Susan called him Mr. Big. I just called him Charlie.

He grinned at me as if he knew what I was thinking—and he probably did. I willed myself not to respond to his fatal charm. We'd been friends for several years, and I knew better than to fall for him. He was one of those slippery fish that always got away.

"You know," Charlie told me as he leaned down to pet the obsequious beagle, "this is one exceptional hound. He's what we call a 'bawler.' Bawlers are the lead howlers of the pack. They're bred to bay."

"Great." I rolled my eyes.

"You'll never break him of it. It's what he was born to do."

I sighed. "Just my luck."

"Actually yes, it is," Charlie said. "A bawler is the hunting dog of hunting dogs. A very special dog. Freddie is worth some serious money."

I laughed. "To whom?"

"To any serious hunter," Charlie said.

"I'll remember that," I told Charlie, wondering if I could sell the boisterous beast on eBay. "Believe me, I'll remember that."

As I watched Charlie drive away later that afternoon, I found myself pondering his bawler beagle theory. Or fact, which I guess it was fact as opposed to theory, at least from the hunter's point of view.

I went back inside and sat down on my couch.

"Come here, Freddie," I said. The little hound trotted over to me, tail wagging. I rubbed his silky ears, and gazed into his soulful eyes. "Charlie says that you are a special dog. With a unique skill worth some serious money. And here I just thought you were a loud-mouthed beagle."

Freddie cocked his head at me. I laughed. "Usually I mistake a male's weakness for strength. But with you, I mistook a strength for weakness. Maybe that's progress."

Or maybe not.

chapter ten

"The fact is that your puppy responds to your emotional state. When you're upset, your puppy gets upset. When you're happy, your puppy tends to be happy."

—PAUL OWENS, *The Puppy Whisperer*

OUR TINY 900-SQUARE-FOOT COTTAGE WAS BURSTING AT THE SEAMS: Mikey, me, Isis the Cat, Shakespeare the Elder, Freddie the Puppy, and nearly fifty pairs of shoes all fighting for space. More if you count the shoes I had to store in the garage for lack of space. Even more if you count the ones I had to throw in the garbage after Freddie chewed them into bits. (In only a few months, it had become clear that, other issues aside, Freddie and I had a couple of things in common. We both loved Mikey—and we both loved shoes. My shoes.)

Crowded quarters and mangled stilettos aside, we were pretty happy. Which is to say that Mikey was happy, so I was happy. All my doubts and fears were fading away. I settled into my new job, Mikey settled into his new school (sans French class). By Thanksgiving, I was secretly congratulating myself on a very successful move. I knew I was right in doing so when Mikey complained about going to California to see his father.

"Do I have to go?" Mikey asked me the Sunday before Turkey Day. We were curled up on the couch, watching the Patriots win another football game. "I just spent all summer at her house. They won't even miss me."

"Your father will miss you." Moving back to Massachusetts had cost me nearly every holiday and all of summer vacation. Most of the time I believed it was worth it. Except, of course, for every holiday and all of summer vacation.

"Mom," Mikey said, making his best case, "the food is terrible."

"How can that be? Nothing's easier than turkey."

"She doesn't cook, Mom. So Dad grills the turkey."

My ex hated food preparation of any kind. He was a man's man, who believed that real women cooked and real men ate what real women cooked—or drove through In-N-Out Burger. The thought of Miss Priss unable to roast a turkey pleased me more than I could say. My ex saddled with a Doppelganger who couldn't cook pleased me more than I could say. Or should say.

"Really!" Really is what I always say when I can't trust myself to say anything else.

"The stuffing is disgusting."

"Your father makes stuffing?" Now I was pissed. How dare he learn to make stuffing. I was the stuffing maker in my son's life.

"No. Some old lady always makes it. And it's disgusting."

"I'm sorry, honey. But I'll make you a real Thanksgiving dinner when you get back." I gave him a big hug, which he wriggled out of as soon as he thought he could without hurting my feelings. I could practically hear him counting to ten in his head.

Freddie bounded over, always quick to worm his way into any familial show of affection, whether intended for him or not. Mikey scooped him up and cradled him like the big baby he was. "What about Freddie, Mom?"

"I'll take good care of him. I promise." And I would. As long as he didn't destroy any more of my shoes.

"I wish I could take him with me."

"That wouldn't be very practical." I paused. "Besides, it's your father's call," I added, knowing full well he'd never spring for the extra fare.

"Dad would never pay for it." Mikey sighed, and scratched Freddie's puppy potbelly. "Freddie would hate it there, anyway."

"Why do you say that? Don't they have a dog?"

"They're mean to their dog. Ginger never gets to come inside."

"That doesn't sound like your father at all." Mikey's dad had his faults, but even I had to grant that mistreating animals was not one of them.

"They say she's too wild. So they make her stay outside all day and all night. They never pay any attention to her."

"Poor Ginger." I reached over and scratched Freddie's belly myself. Sometimes I really loved this paunchy little pooch. I smiled. "Well, Freddie likes hanging out in the house. So you'd better just leave him here. You won't be gone long."

"It always *seems* long," Mikey said.

I bit my lip to keep from smirking.

When I took Mikey to the airport, I waited with him at the gate. Since Mikey was "an unaccompanied minor" in airline parlance, I had to secure his boarding pass and get a special security pass for myself. We spent a lot of time at airports together during his short life; he had traveled cross-country on his own since the age of six. I didn't like it very much, but there was really nothing I could do about it. A court order was a court order—and I was in no position legally or financially to defy it.

Every Christmas, winter break, spring break, summer, and Thanksgiving we went through the same rigmarole. I used to pack for him, but now he did it himself. I did insist that he only take old clothes, since whatever he took with him inevitably got thrown together with Miss Priss's boys' stuff. He never came back with what he took with him. No one seemed to know what happened to Mikey's stuff when he was there, even though Miss Priss had a maid who supposedly did all the laundry.

"It's like a black hole over there, Mom," Mikey would say when he came back with a suitcase full of mismatched socks and torn jeans—none of which were his. "I swear."

After spending way too much money on nice new clothes for him to wear on his California jaunts (to prove that I was the best mother in the world with or without a husband), I finally gave up. Mikey didn't protest. When he was little he never cared what he wore here or there; now as he approached adolescence he chose his so-called wardrobe of jeans and shirts very carefully—and didn't want to lose anything.

Even though he packed for himself now we still went through the same checklist on the day of departure.

"Do you have your passport?" We'd gotten Mikey a passport when we went to Europe to visit his sister Alexis when he was in the sixth grade, and now it served as his identification when he traveled. Without it, he wasn't going anywhere.

"Yes, Mom."

"Let me see it." Just because he said he had it didn't mean he actually had it.

"I've got it, Mom."

"I need to physically see it. Remember that time we drove halfway to the airport and you didn't have it?" We had to go all the way back home, get the passport, and then get to the airport before the plane left for California. I didn't want to be put in the position of telling his father that we'd missed the flight, so I drove like a bat out of hell that day.

"Okay, okay, here it is. See?"

"Toothbrush?"

"Yeah."

"Underwear?"

"Yeah."

"Book?"

"Yeah."

"Read it this time, will you?"

"Uh huh. . . . Can we go now, Mom?"

But he never read the book. And there was always a book he was supposed to read for English class, even in the summer. In fact, there was a whole list of books he was supposed to read every summer. But it never happened. I bought him the books, but just like his clothes they disappeared into the black hole. As a mom I found this dismaying; as a book editor I took it as a personal affront. Mikey claimed there were no books at her house, and that her boys couldn't read. Whether he said this to fuel my disdain or simply to explain why he played video games all summer rather than read the assigned books, I wasn't sure.

There are two kinds of people in the world: the people who arrive way too early for a flight, and the people who arrive nearly too late. I'm one of the early people. Which means that we always had plenty of time once we got to the airport. Time enough for our ritual bowl of clam chowder at Legal Sea Foods, and time enough for Mikey to realize that he didn't have the book he's supposed to read, after all.

"Mom," Mikey said as we finished up our chowder, "I forgot the book."

"Great." I called for the check. "Well, the good news is that every decent bookstore in America carries *To Kill a Mockingbird*. I'm sure the Borders here will have it in paperback. Let's go."

Mikey sighed. A trip to the bookstore is an adventure for me— and hell for him. Yet we always ended up there every time we went to the airport. (Secretly I thought that proved that there was hope for the kid, after all.) At the bookstore I morphed into work mode, *To Kill a Mockingbird* forgotten. I combed through the shelves, checking all the books on promotion, on the front tables and the end caps. They sold a lot of books in airports—and I always checked the stores to see which of the books I'd acquired and edited were stocked on the shelves. I counted them.

"Mom, we've got to go." Mikey was not browsing the bookstore, he was playing his Game Boy, rocking back and forth on his heels as he thumbed the device. He looked up at me. "Come on, Mom."

"Okay." I pulled myself away from the face-out new nonfiction display at the front of the store. "Did you get the book?"

"No."

I sighed, loudly.

"You're the one who knows where to look, Mom."

True enough. I dragged him over to the *L*s in the fiction section, and pulled out a mass-market copy of the classic by Harper Lee. Only $12.95. *Sold.*

"Okay. Now don't lose this one."

Mikey rolled his eyes. I paid for his book, and got the new Alice Hoffman for myself. We got back to the gate and still had an hour to kill. I pulled out my book and gave Mikey his.

"This is a great book, you know," I told him. "You should read it."

Mikey kept on playing his Game Boy. "We're going to watch the movie in class."

"Great movie, too," I said. "You know I named your brother after Gregory Peck in that movie."

"That's so lame, Mom."

"No, it's not." I glared at him. "You still need to read the book. Starting now." I glared at him again until he picked up the book and began to read.

We both read our respective novels until they announced that it was time to board the plane. The flight attendant came for Mikey, and I gave him a big hug. This time he didn't resist, but held on tight for a long moment. When he finally pulled away, he said, "Take good care of Freddie, Mom."

"I will, love." I ruffled his brown curls as he turned to follow the flight attendant. I watched him go, and willed away the tears that gathered at the back of my eyes. There is something so forlorn about a little boy flying solo across the nation, his backpack thrown over one shoulder, his boarding pass and passport tucked in the plastic holder hanging around his neck, the little airline pin on his collar proclaiming to the world that *I am a child of divorce whose parents weren't grown up enough to raise me together as is the natural course of things.*

"Watch out for that stuffing," I called after him.

Now came the part I always hated most. I had to wait in the airport until Mikey's plane was in the air before I could leave the airport, per airline regulations. Sensible regulations, but they afforded me plenty of time to watch other whole, intact families happily traveling together on national holidays. Parents who didn't send their young sons off on their own with nothing but a passport, a Game Boy, and a copy of *To Kill a Mockingbird.* (Although if you could only choose one book for the road, that *was* a good one.)

Waiting tonight would be somewhat easier for me than usual. Sure, I'd still have to sit here surrounded by the Traveling Cleavers with nothing but Alice Hoffman for support. But I wouldn't have to go back alone, thinking about how my choices had ruined my children on the long drive home to Lytton. I'd arranged for my older son Greg to fly in on the same airline about an hour after Mikey's flight was due to depart. He was coming home for Thanksgiving—and longer, if I could talk him into it.

Gregory Paul: my middle child. Anyone with three or more children knows what that means: *Trouble.*

Entertaining and endearing, but trouble nonetheless. Greg's grandmother Lilly once told me that the child who gives you the most trouble was the one you ended up loving the most.

"Because you work the hardest on the one who's the most trouble," she confided.

At the time I was horrified that she would say such a thing, and thought she was simply serving up a rationalization for the way she coddled her middle child, my first husband—who as it turned out was far more trouble for all of us than Greg could ever hope to be.

I was an only child, who'd enjoyed the sole attention of my adoring parents from day one, and knew nothing yet of sibling rivalry or (perceived) parental favoritism. I wanted children so badly and was thrilled to have them that I could not imagine preferring one over the other. I loved all my children equally, and each had a special claim on my mother's heart.

Alexis was my first-born princess, my only girl, the light of my life who'd been diagnosed with Type 1 diabetes at only thirteen, thereby clinching my overprotection for life.

Mikey was my youngest, the third child I never expected to have, the miracle baby conceived as a result of the vasectomy reversal my second husband underwent the year he turned forty.

And Greg was my middle child, the personality kid who always made me laugh, just like his father, my first husband, had. And without a doubt the one I worked the hardest on.

And I had more work to do. I could see that from where I stood at the base of the escalators in Terminal B, watching as my handsome son descended home to me once more. But Greg didn't look good. His broad shoulders were hunched, his dark blond hair disheveled. His blue eyes were bloodshot and deepened by dark shadows; he needed a shave. His forearms were pocked with eczema, a telltale sign of stress. There was a shrouded look about him, a shutting down I recognized immediately.

I walked toward him, my arms outstretched, my smiling face hiding my alarm at his physical and emotional state.

"Darling boy."

"Mommy." He hugged me, and held on even tighter and longer than his little brother had just an hour before.

When the kids were little, we called it "re-entry." After every visit with their father, Alexis and Greg would come home as exhausted and disoriented as astronauts returning from outer space. And like the astronauts they required a mandatory recovery period. The longer the visit, the longer the recovery period. Alexis would curl up in a fetal ball on my lap, and not move for at least twenty-four hours. Greg would bounce off the walls, full of a frenetic energy that defied all of my efforts to ground him again. So I would just be there for them both, letting them unwind until they were ready to live by Mom's house rules again.

At the time I chalked their behavior up to the normal displacement caused by shuttling back and forth between two very different parents and households—the re-entry phenomenon was in all the books I'd read on children and divorce—but in retrospect that was very naive on my part. Of course I knew that their brilliant, successful father could be self-absorbed and scatterbrained—my father had dubbed him the "absent-minded professor" back when he was still in graduate school—but I had no idea how troubled he had become. Twenty years later I knew better—the stories of his losing battles with substance abuse and mental illness were now the stuff of family legend—and feared for my son's emotional health.

"Let's go home," I said gently to my sweet, sensitive middle child. "You can meet Freddie."

"Freddie?" Greg looked confused.

"Mikey's new puppy."

"Oh, yeah." Greg smiled. "Right. Mikey told me about him. I guess I forgot."

"You look tired, love. Let's get you home."

On the way back to the lake, the flurries began. Greg fell asleep along the way, for which I was grateful. I knew that he sometimes suffered from insomnia, especially when he was living with his dad. Dealing with his erratic, often manic father was a round-the-clock job—as physically taxing as it was emotionally taxing. Greg needed to sleep—and I was glad that he could.

By the time we pulled into the driveway in front of the house, more than an inch of snow covered the ground. By the time I tucked my tired son into his little brother's bed, the white stuff was piling up fast, blanketing the cottage and drifting high under the eaves.

Isis crept into the room, took a graceful leap, and made an elegant landing on the pillow next to Greg's head. The persnickety tabby stepped carefully onto Greg's chest, then curled into a tight ball right above my boy's heart. She had an unerring compassion that always manifested itself at the lowest times in her people's lives. During the divorce, she'd spent many a night on my chest.

Freddie jumped onto the covers, and burrowed into Greg's backside.

"Jeez, dog!" Greg rolled over. "Mom, can you take him? You know I'm allergic."

Shakespeare stood stoically at my side, watching Greg.

"You're far more allergic to Isis," I reminded him. "You'll have to get used to the animals again. In the meantime, I'll get the allergy pills for you—and take Isis with me."

I reached for the cat and pulled her carefully off Greg and onto my shoulder.

"Freddie sleeps with Mikey," I told Greg as I left the room. "Shakespeare and Isis sleep with me. So I guess now Freddie sleeps with you. At least until your brother gets back and you get kicked to the couch."

I brought Greg a glass of water and the allergy pills, kissed his forehead, and said goodnight. I closed the door behind me, leaving Greg and Freddie to their respective dreams. Shakespeare, Isis, and I settled in my bedroom, and we all fell asleep to the howling of the wind in the first big storm of the season. For once, it wasn't Freddie.

"Mom!" Greg stood above me in the dark as I lie sleeping in my bed. Trying to sleep, anyway.

"Mom, wake up!"

I sat up on my elbows. "Honey, what's the matter? What time is it?"

"He got out, Mom."

"What?" I noticed the cigarette that hung from Greg's lips. "Why are you smoking in the house? It's no good for you. And you know there's no smoking in the house."

"I was not smoking in the house, Mom. I was outside." Greg pulled the cigarette from his mouth and looked around for the ashtray he'd never find in my house.

"In this weather?" The snowstorm had gathered force during the night, turning into a full-scale blizzard.

"I went out on the back porch, just like you told me to." Greg started smoking in high school. He quit after college, but whenever he was stressed out, he would start up again. After living with his father in Florida, he was back up to two packs a day. "I mean, that's how it happened."

"What happened?" Now I was fully awake and on alert.

"Freddie came out on the porch with me—and then he took off."

I was out of bed now, slipping my robe over my flannel pajamas. "You let him loose on the porch?" The back porch was screened—and full of big holes after the heavy rains of summer and the high winds of autumn.

"I didn't know he could get out, Mom." Greg gave up looking for an ashtray, and put the cigarette back into his mouth. "I'm sorry."

"It's okay, honey. I should have warned you about Freddie." I pulled my boots on over my slippers, and my dad's old parka over my robe. "We have to find him. He'll freeze out there."

I started rummaging through the kitchen cabinets, looking for a flashlight. "We'll need a flashlight." I slammed a drawer. "Why can I never find a flashlight when I need one? Maybe in the garage . . . come on, Shakespeare." I turned to Greg. "You stay here, in case he finds his way home. Call me on my cell if that happens." I opened the door to a rush of wind-borne snow. "That's assuming we even get phone service in this gale."

"But, Mom—"

"I'll be fine. I'll have Shakespeare with me," I was yelling now, to be heard over the howling of the wind. "If I'm not back in an hour, call in the cavalry." I pushed the door shut behind me with my back, pulled the parka hood tightly over my head, and headed out into the whiteout with Shakespeare. One look at the garage and I knew I'd be without a flashlight. The snow had drifted some four feet high against the door, blocking entry.

The snow came nearly to my knees, just below the line of my boots. I trudged along, Shakespeare at my side. Shakespeare may hate the rain, but he loved the snow. They said he was a mutt when we got him, a sheepdog mix of unknown origin, but I knew better. Sure, he obviously had sheepdog in him, any fool could see that. But after much research I believed that he had to be a Catalan sheepdog, a rare breed from the Catalonia region of Spain known for its good nature, superior herding skill, and general sturdiness. Also known as the *Gos d'Atura Català*, these rugged, friendly dogs were built to withstand the outdoors, even in the winter. They loved the snow— and could spend hours outside even in the worst of frosty weather. I stood by my canine identification, but even if Shakespeare weren't 100 percent Catalan sheepdog, he was definitely 100 percent snow dog. The very best companion to venture out into a blizzard with at two in the morning.

Between the black liquid darkness of the night and the pure white blindness of the storm, visibility was virtually nil. Shakespeare and I pushed forward against the spitting wind.

"Freddie!" I called, not in the high-pitched yodel with which I lured him in from the frozen pond, but in a megaphone bellow that could possibly be heard over the nor'easter. "Freddie!"

I stomped on, shaking the ice off my boots with every step. Shakespeare bounded ahead, if you could call wading hip deep in snow bounding. He barked along with my deep keening and together we made our way in the general direction of the road. The frigid gusts cut right through the thick layers of parka, terrycloth, flannel, and chilled me beyond the bone. Even Shakespeare with his copious shaggy coat stopped occasionally to shudder, sending snow and ice flying.

"Freddie! Freddie!" I called and called until my throat stung. We hadn't gotten very far, maybe a quarter of a mile. It was very slow going when the snow was this deep. Not to mention an exhausting plod—like cross-country skiing without the skis. After twenty minutes I was beginning to rethink this search for Freddie. I couldn't see anything. I couldn't hear anything. I certainly couldn't find anything. But I couldn't abandon the search either. I couldn't leave Mikey's little lost beagle out in the cold to die. So I kept on clomping along, head bowed against the wind. Shakespeare seemed to understand, as he always did, and cantered along besides me, as elegantly as was possible in such snowy chaos.

I grew very tired, and my thoughts inevitably turned to that Frost poem that ends so badly, *Stopping by Woods on a Snowy Evening*. I may have miles to go as well—but how far could Freddie have gone? He was much shorter than Shakespeare, a little tank of a puppy who would sink in these drifts like a stone. He couldn't have roamed very far in this weather—and he surely couldn't have made better time.

I needed to think like a dog. Where would a hound crazy enough to go out in a blizzard go? That's when I realized my mistake. Freddie would not stick to the road, as I was doing. He'd head right for the woods. Because that's where his nose would lead him. I turned around and headed back down to the curve in the road where the woods met our street for the first time. Shakespeare apparently approved of this change in direction; he vaulted into the woods without hesitation. I picked my way after him, trudging through the tall pines carefully, watching for low limbs. The woods ran in a narrow line between our road and the next road over, flanked by the backyards along each sparse row of houses.

When I came out the other side, I stepped into a clearing that I knew must be one of these yards. Shakespeare led the charge onto the snow-covered lawn. Abruptly the big dog stopped short, bushy ears at attention.

That's when I heard it. Above the din of the storm, the unmistakable howl of an unhappy hound.

"Freddie!" I screamed with as much relief as joy. "Freddie!"

As if in answer, the yowling intensified, ringing clear as a beagle's bell through the blinding snow. I stumbled down an icy slope into an unexpectedly deep bank of snow toward that wonderful, terrible screeching. Shakespeare disappeared into the whiteout before me, adding his baritone bark to the growing racket.

And suddenly there he was: a shivering, squalling ball of soggy fur, spotlighted by a motion sensor under the back deck of a large Cape Cod house. Excited, Freddie lunged toward me over and over again, but got nowhere. He was stuck.

Shakespeare leaped into Freddie's limelight, and sniffed the wayward puppy. I ran the last few yards, my boots catching in the snow, my feet growing wetter and colder with each and every step.

Freddie's collar was caught on a nail. The shivering beagle was immobilized.

"How did you manage to do this?" I asked him. Then I spied the trashcan at his feet. "Well, that explains it." With nearly frozen fingers I freed the collar from the nail and snapped on the leash. Freddie jumped up on me, sloppy tail wagging, baying all the while.

I leaned over and patted the pathetic pooch, rubbing his frosty fur with my gloved hands to warm him.

"Okay," I said, "let's get you home." I stood up against the wind and prepared to press onward home.

"Come on," I yelled at the dogs. "Let's go home."

And the three of us tramped back through the woods and down the road to our little cottage dressed in Christmas lights, which shone in the storm like the lovely beacon it was.

For all of us, Greg included.

Quick Fix: *noun*, a short-term and/or insufficient solution

chapter eleven

"It is very difficult to contain a beagle with the time and motivation to engineer escapes."

—LAURIE KRAMER, *BeaglesontheWeb.com*

*H*OWLING. *"ACCIDENTS." CHEWING SHOES AND CABINETS AND books (My shoes! My cabinets! My books!).* If all that weren't enough, it appeared that just as with adolescence in humans, the typical beagle's adolescence is also characterized by challenging and escaping parental authority wherever and whenever possible.

For Freddie, this desire to escape was more than drive, more than inclination, more than sport. It was a primal obsession driven by a nose that wouldn't—couldn't!—stop sniffing, tracking, hunting. *Escaping.*

Any living creature with a proboscis has nasal tissue covered with receptors designed to "capture" smells. We humans have some 6 million of these sites. Dogs have millions more. The better the nose, the more the receptors. Sheepdogs have some 200 million. Guess how many Freddie has? 300 million! This bears repeating: the average beagle's nose boasts 300 million olfactory receptors designed to capture the odors of the universe.

Scientists say that the beagle's sense of smell is conceivably *millions of times* more acute than ours. They "smell" the world with the same clarity with which we humans "see" the world. And they do it faster, since smell transmits to the brain more quickly than sight or sound.

Knowing all this helped me understand why Freddie—and *not* Shakespeare—would tear the couch apart to get to the one lone piece of popcorn tucked far beneath a sofa cushion. Or drag a pan of freshly baked brownies off the counter and gobble them up in a few big gulps. Or break into the "dog-proof" trash receptacle to consume the carcass of our roast chicken supper. It did not help me buy a new couch. It did not help me bake new brownies. It did not help me pick up the trash.

And it didn't help me find Freddie when he managed to break out of the cottage and head for the hills. Or deep woods or cranberry bogs or salt marshes, as the case may be. For Freddie, there was a world of good smells within the walls of our cozy cottage—and a universe of good smells beyond them. And he seemed hound-bound to explore them all.

After that snowy scare the night he arrived, Greg tried to be more careful, but taking care was never his forte. As distraction was his natural state, my middle child inevitably became an unwitting if unwilling accomplice to Freddie's escape artistry. He quickly bonded with the boisterous beagle, with whom he shared a fated flair for trouble.

"He's so cute, Mom," Greg said to me the next morning. He pulled Freddie to his lap, scratching the pooch's protruding belly. "Beagles are *such* cute dogs. I really think that they're the cutest dogs of all."

"Don't let Shakespeare hear you say that," I said. We were home now, alone together at the cottage for the bulk of the Thanksgiving holiday while Mikey was out in California.

"Dad had a beagle," Greg said. "His name was Sammy. I loved that dog."

"Right." Of course the dog he remembered was the dog he had

while he lived in hell with his father, not Rambo, the fabulous rottweiler–Great Dane mix my dad and I got him when he was a kid. I didn't say anything; I was used to taking a back seat to his father in my older son's psyche, if not his heart. My first husband was a funny, smart force of nature, a bona fide genius whose brilliance was compromised by his on-again, off-again substance abuse and mental instability. Greg had spent several years of his young life trying to save his father from himself.

This last time was particularly brutal. After Greg graduated from Hunter College in New York City, his father invited him down to Fort Lauderdale to "learn the business." (That is, the investment banking business, as practiced by an erratic mastermind.) But Greg wound up doing what he always wound up doing: babysitting an increasingly desperate and disturbed man intent on destroying himself. These periods always ended badly, with his father in the hospital and Greg with nowhere to go but home to Mom.

"Dad loved that dog, too," Greg said.

"Right."

"Really, Mom. It was funny to see Dad taking care of Sammy. He babied him."

I couldn't even manage a "Right" to that. In my experience, the man couldn't take care of anyone, including himself. What's more, he didn't even want to. "What happened to him?"

"Huh?"

"The beagle. Your dad's dog, Sammy."

"I don't know." Greg frowned. "You never know what happens with anything with Dad."

Now that was the man I knew and (used to) love, I thought to myself. Aloud I said, "You know, honey, you can't keep on doing this." I squeezed my boy's shoulder. "You can't save your father. You need to let him go—and build a life for yourself."

Greg nuzzled Freddie. "I know, Mom, but I honestly don't know where to begin."

"You have to start right where you are, decide where you want to go, and just put one foot in front of the other until you get there."

"But what can I do, Mom?"

"You can do anything you want to do."

"You always say that, Mom. But it's not true." Greg sighed. "I can't do anything. Maybe I should get an MBA."

"Oh, honey, you'll die of boredom in business school."

"Maybe." Greg thought about that. "I could always go to law school."

I groaned. "The last thing the world needs is more lawyers." As a woman who'd been divorced twice, I didn't think much of lawyers. "Besides, anybody can be a lawyer. You have an original mind. You need to do something creative."

"You always say that, Mom," Greg said again. "But it's not—"

"I always say it because it's true," I said. Greg was correct. We'd had this conversation before, most notably before he went down to Florida to learn the investment-banking business. Greg thought in doing so he'd be getting a *real* job that would allow him to make *real* money. I thought it would just make him *really* miserable—as it had his father before him.

I'd met my first husband at Purdue University in the seventies. I was an undergrad; he was a brilliant graduate student, with a promising future ahead of him. He was the most fascinating man I'd ever met—a poet, a musician, a composer, a linguist, a champion chess player, a political scientist, a scholar, a rebel.

When we married, I thought I was hitching my star to a gifted artist. But instead of following his bliss, he followed the money. He put his dreams aside, became an investment banker, and began a long slide into madness.

I did not want that to happen to my son Greg, who shared many of his father's talents.

"You can write, you can tell stories, you can make people laugh. If you insist on going back to graduate school, then study something useful. Go to film school."

Greg shook his head, laughing. "You're the only mom in America who tells her son to go to film school instead of getting an MBA or a law degree."

"I just want you to be happy. I've worked with a lot of MBAs and a lot of lawyers—and none of them is happy."

"Come on, Mom."

"Seriously. They all want to be writers." I looked at my son. "You already are a writer." Greg had written a book for my former employer.

"I wrote one book, Mom. And you rewrote most of it for me. That doesn't make me a writer."

"You are, too, a writer," I said in my severest mom voice. "Of course you needed help. Everyone needs help writing their first book. That's why God made editors."

Greg laughed. "And mothers." His smile faded. "You got me the job. I'd never have gotten a book contract if my mom weren't in publishing. Everyone knows that."

I shrugged. "If I were a plumber, I'd teach you to plumb. But I'm a writer, so I teach my kids to write. You wrote a book, your sister wrote a book. Maybe someday Mikey will write a book, too. There's nothing unusual in that. It's in your genes."

"If you say so."

"You've been through a lot, sweetie," I said. "You need a break. You have plenty of time to decide what you do next. In the meantime, we'll come up with another book for you to write."

So that's what we did. I talked Greg into staying with us until he got back on his feet—or forever if that's what he wanted. Mikey came home after Thanksgiving and was thrilled to learn that his big brother would be around for the foreseeable future. I knew it would be good for them both. Not to mention good for me; I was so happy to have both my boys with me again. I'd long resigned myself to my older children growing up and leaving home; it was, after all, what they were supposed to do. But with my daughter Alexis living happily ever after abroad, it was wonderful to have Greg at home, if only for a little while.

While I was at work and Mikey was at school, Greg stayed at the cottage with Freddie and Shakespeare and Isis, working on a new book. Freddie became Greg's muse. The lively little beagle kept Greg company while he wrote, and Greg kept the lively little beagle from destroying the house. It was a symbiotic relationship.

Having Greg around was good for Mikey and me, too. Greg provided Mikey with a brotherly shoulder to lean on—and stepped in as the best friend he needed until he forged his own close friendships with the kids at his new school. As for me, well, I was always thrilled to have my older children at home again. Once they grew up and went out on their own, I didn't see that much of them. And I missed them. Greg had always been my funny child, the one who learned early on that if you made me laugh, I'd forgive you anything. Even at my most stressed, Greg could always make me laugh.

That said, leaving the boys and the dogs at home alone to their own devices sometimes spelled disaster. Greg's absentmindedness coupled with Mikey's general adolescent cluelessness meant that Freddie could escape into the wild more frequently, if he acted quickly when the opportunity presented itself. And Freddie was nothing if not an opportunist.

One cold, clear evening not long after Thanksgiving I came home from work to find Freddie and Shakespeare waiting for me right by the door on the front deck, their respective leashes still attached to their collars, their coats slick with slush. A brief spell of unseasonably warm weather had melted much of the snow, but a thick layer of icy sludge remained. The winter sun set early so it was very dark at the cottage by the time I got home at six o'clock. Out here by the lake there were no street lamps. What ambient light there was came from the moon, the stars that shone in the night sky overhead, and the porch lights of the houses scattered along the lakeshore.

The boys were nowhere to be found. I let the impatient dogs in the house, and called Greg on his cell. But it went straight to voice mail. I left a message asking him to call me to let me know what was going on, and went into my bedroom to slip out of my work clothes and into jeans and a sweater. My favorite quilt, the aquamarine and cobalt blue one with the Lady of the Lake pattern, was missing from my bed. Which I thought was odd, but as I had the missing boys on my mind, I decided to figure that one out later and concentrate on making dinner.

I'd roasted a large capon for supper the night before, so I thought I'd whip up a little chicken fettuccine with the leftovers. But the chicken was missing as well. This was not the surprise it could have been; when you had boys in the house food vanished without a crumb as rapidly as you prepared it. There was no such thing as a full larder with Greg and Mikey here—and I knew that. I usually warned them not to eat whatever I was planning to cook for dinner, but those warnings often went unheeded. I poked around the freezer and came up with some hamburger I could defrost in the microwave and whip up into my special male-pleasing mini-meatloaves in minutes.

An hour later dinner was ready—and the boys still weren't home. I was getting worried. Just as I was about to call the police, I heard a commotion out on the street side of the cottage. Freddie and Shakespeare bounded for the front door, yelping.

In came the boys, cold and muddy and wet.

"They're *here*?" Greg looked at me, then at Mikey, then at the dogs. "The dogs are *here*?"

Mikey shrugged. "They're here." He squatted down to hug Freddie, who licked the melted snow from his face.

"How long have they been here?" asked Greg.

"I don't know. They were waiting here at the front door when I got home." I pointed to the kitchen table where dinner was laid out, waiting for my family to sit down and eat it. The boys clamored into their seats, and I poured Greg and myself each a large glass of red wine. I had a feeling we both needed it.

In between mouthfuls of meatloaf, the boys filled me in on their little adventure.

"We were just taking the dogs on a walk through the bogs," Greg said. "Like you told me to do, Mom."

"Greg needs the exercise," Mikey said.

Greg punched his little brother in the arm. "Shut up."

"That's what you said, jerk-face."

"Moron."

"Idiot."

"Ass—"

"That's enough." I knew that this crass brotherly one-upmanship could go on indefinitely. "Back to your story."

"Okay," Greg said. "We were walking through the bogs, and a couple of Mikey's friends came along, and we got distracted and the next thing we knew . . . ."

Greg went on, but I didn't really hear him. He had me at "a couple of Mikey's friends." Mikey had friends?

"What friends?"

"What?"

"What *friends*?"

"You know, the guys. Jo Jo and Brian and Ross and Wilbur." Mikey rattled off the names of boys I'd never heard of before, but was delighted to hear about now.

"That's wonderful, honey!"

"Back to the dogs," Greg said to us both.

"Mom, you're not listening." Mikey frowned. "We lost the dogs in the bogs."

"Shakespeare, too?"

"Yeah." Greg sipped his wine. "Freddie took off like a bat out of hell and Shakespeare went right along with him."

"That's weird," I said. "Freddie typically acts alone. Usually Shakespeare is better behaved."

"It was all Greg's fault," Mikey mumbled, his mouth full of meatloaf.

"Not true," Greg said. "They just took off, Mom—"

"You chased Freddie. Everyone knows you don't chase a running dog." Mikey looked at me. "They just run harder. Even Shakespeare." Mikey sighed. "Right, Mom?"

"How are you supposed to catch them if you don't chase them?"

Mikey rolled his eyes at his older brother. "You just *call* them, dipstick."

"Nimrod."

"Schmuck."

"That's enough." I glared at Greg. "Watch your language around your little brother."

"Yeah." Greg snorted. "Like he's never heard it before."

"Even so," I warned.

"I'm telling you, Mom, he's got some mouth on him for twelve."

"Oh, please," Mikey said. "We all know what you were doing at twelve."

"Yeah." Greg grinned. "I was doing what you only *wish* you were doing."

Mikey reached over and punched his big brother on the arm.

"So you chased the dogs through the bogs," I interjected. My mom radar was beginning to kick in. "Where do my roast chicken and my favorite quilt come in?"

Greg and Mikey exchanged a sheepish glance.

"'Fess up," I said.

"You know how the bogs run into that forest at the south end?" asked Mikey.

I nodded. "Yes, I do."

"Well, that's where Greg chased them, into the woods."

"I didn't *chase* them into the woods," Greg said. "I *followed* them."

"Freddie goes where his nose leads him," I said to Mikey. "He's right about that."

"Whatever," said Mikey.

"Go on." I poured myself another generous glass of wine. I figured it was going to be another long night.

"We were deep in the forest," Greg intoned, as if this were the heavily forested Green Mountains of Vermont rather than a suburban wood on the South Shore of Massachusetts.

"We were *lost*," said Mikey.

"We weren't lost," said Greg. "But there was no sign of the dogs."

"No sign at all," chimed in Mikey.

"But then we ran into this old guy," said Greg. "Creepy guy with a graying ponytail, dressed in dirty camouflage. I think he was a survivalist."

"He was homeless, dude."

"He had a tent," Greg said. "I'm betting it was full of guns."

"Guns!" I looked at Mikey. "What guns?"

"We never saw any guns, Mom," Mikey said. "Greg, tell Mom we never saw any guns."

"We didn't actually *see* any guns," Greg conceded. "But—"

"We asked him if he'd seen the dogs," said Mikey.

"And he said no," Greg said.

"He's the one who told us to get the chicken and the quilt," said Mikey.

"You took advice from some gun-toting adventurer you found in a tent in the woods?" I shook my head.

"Homeless person," Mikey said.

"Survivalist," Greg countered.

"Whatever," said Mikey.

"He said we should go home and get some of the dogs' favorite food," said Mikey.

"That explains where our dinner went," I said.

"Freddie does love chicken, Mom," Mikey said.

"True enough," I said. This wasn't the first roast chicken with Freddie's name on it that had disappeared. "But what about my Lady of the Lake quilt?"

"Lady of the Lake?" Greg asked.

"It's the name of the quilt pattern," I explained.

"Because Mom's a lady who lives on a lake," Mikey said, rolling his eyes. "Get it?"

"I get it," Greg said, rolling his eyes as well. "No great loss there, Mom."

"I loved that quilt! That's not an easy pattern to find, you know."

The boys started to laugh at me, then thought better of it when they caught sight of the "you're grounded for life" expression on my motherly face.

"The guy said we should get a blanket or something from home," Mikey said.

"Why didn't you use your own blanket then?" I asked. "Or one of my good Egyptian cotton towels?"

"Very funny, Mom." Mikey sighed.

"He said that it had to be something that smelled like someone the dogs love," said Greg.

Mikey looked down his nose at me. "You know the dogs love you best, Mom."

"That's not true. They just know who brings home the bacon." I paused. "So you came home, got the chicken and my Lady of the Lake quilt, and then went back into the woods?"

"Yeah," said Greg. "But we still couldn't find them."

"So why didn't you just bring it all back home?"

"Greg got scared," Mikey said.

"I did not."

Mikey laughed. "You did, too!"

"Dipstick."

"Moron."

"Idiot."

I started to laugh.

"It was getting dark." Greg looked at me. "We heard some strange noises."

I hyperventilated.

"Greg thought the homeless guy was going to kill us," Mikey said.

"I'm telling you, he was a *survivalist*," said Greg. "He came out of the tent waving a gun at us."

"It wasn't a gun, it was a stick," Mikey said.

"Whatever." Greg stared hard at his little brother. "You were as scared as I was. Admit it."

Mikey bowed his head. "I dropped the chicken and ran for home."

"I dropped the quilt and ran after him," Greg said.

I gasped for breath between guffaws. The boys laughed, too. And then we all ate ice cream.

The next day I bought myself a new spread for my antique iron bed, a colorful patchwork of calico and velvet and satin in the Crazy Quilt pattern, which seemed far more appropriate given the current circumstances of my life.

chapter twelve

"Standing straight, with your shoulders squared, rather than slumped, can mean the difference between whether your dog obeys a command or ignores it."

—MALCOLM GLADWELL, *What the Dog Saw*

FREDDIE ESCAPED WHENEVER HE COULD, BUT HE ALWAYS FOUND HIS way home again. In that respect he was just like all the rest of us. Escape was a running theme in our family. My daughter Alexis escaped us all after college, and found her way to Europe, making her home there. Greg escaped his father, and found his way back to us again, but whether he'd make his home here permanently remained to be seen. Mikey and I escaped from California, and found our way back to Massachusetts. Now we had a real home of our own here on the lake, but it was a long—and hard and painful and expensive—time coming.

The months that followed that terrible day when we landed in San Tadeo for the family reconciliation that wasn't were a blessed blur to me now—and I hoped for Mikey as well. But at the time we thought we might never recover—or escape.

I did everything I could to help my seven-year-old son and myself adapt to our new circumstances, however unfortunate. With a lot of love and patience and therapy, we survived the constant interaction with my ex and his new family. Mikey was the odd man out at Miss Priss's house during his weekly visits there, but we coped. Just barely, we coped.

We lived in the mother-in-law apartment of a big house nestled at the base of the Santa Cruz Mountains with Isis the cat. Shakespeare was living with the Colonel in Las Vegas, as we couldn't find anyone here who would rent an apartment to a single mom, a boy, a cat, *and* a dog. It was hard enough—not to mention expensive—to find a place that would allow the cat. As it was I was paying $2,000 a month for what amounted to a dump in a very upscale neighborhood known for its good educational system so Mikey could go to a decent school.

We did everything we could to fashion a sunny life there, even in the long shadow of my ex and his new family. We tried to keep our minds on other things. Mikey played field hockey; he took karate lessons; he joined the Boy Scouts. I joined a writer's group; I learned to make mosaics out of broken plates; I took up horseback riding. We went out to dinner with old friends; we drove over the mountains to the beach; we went skiing up at Lake Tahoe. Alexis and Greg and my folks all came to visit. We kept busy, we coped, we talked through our fears and frustrations with the counselor every week. And over time we cried ourselves to sleep a little less often.

And then the dot-com bubble burst. Disney shut down operations at Go.com, and I was out of a job. I went to work for another dot-com, only to be laid off again when that company closed its doors. Silicon Valley went bust again—not for the first time, and not for the last. Northern California was awash in the unemployed, myself included.

I had no choice but to go back to the book business. Unfortunately, there were thousands of people like me who'd left publishing for new Internet companies, lured by six-figure salaries and stock options and the sweet promise of the Golden State. We all wanted our old jobs back—but the positions were few and far between and the competition was fierce. In August 2001, I lucked out and was offered the last job in publishing, acquiring decorating books for a fine-arts publisher in New England. I took it.

Mikey and I left the fabled realm of broken dreams, and escaped for the second time in as many years to the Commonwealth of Massachusetts, upright land of Walden Pond and the Boston Red Sox and wicked good *chowda*. We'd fallen in love with all those wicked good things when we'd escaped to Massachusetts the *first* time, right after my quickie Vegas divorce—and it felt good to embrace them all once again. So we put the big disappointments and little despondencies of the past eighteen months behind us and went back to the unlikely locale we were beginning to think of as home: New England.

It was Labor Day weekend, and we were in Manchester-by-the-Sea on the North Shore, looking for somewhere to live that was relatively close to my new job in Rockport. We needed a home fast, as school was starting and my job was waiting and our furniture was already making its way across the continent.

"It's my turn to pick the place where we live," Mikey said. "And I like this one." Mikey had never much liked the dark basement apartment in California; there really wasn't much to like about it. We were both hoping for something better here.

We stood in a light-filled second-floor apartment down the street from an excellent elementary school—and only a block from one of the most beautiful beaches in the state. The flat was a little smaller than I'd wanted, but perfect in every other way. At any rate, far superior to where we'd lived in San Tadeo: lighter, airier, happier.

We told the real-estate agent we wanted the place, and she sent us to a nearby restaurant to eat lunch, fill out the paperwork, and sign the lease while she ran a credit report. We had just ordered our French dip sandwiches at the local deli when my cell phone rang.

"This is it," I told Mikey. "Fingers crossed." I knew how biased landlords could be against single moms and I wasn't counting on anything.

"Is this Paula Munier?"

"Yes," I said, saying a silent prayer for the apartment.

But it wasn't the landlord calling to announce that we'd gotten the apartment, after all. It was law enforcement.

"We need to inform you that unless you bring your son back to California immediately, you could be arrested by the FBI for kidnapping." The police officer's voice on the other end of the line was kind but firm.

"What?"

The police officer repeated himself. But all I heard was the acronym. Each letter hit me hard: F . . . B . . . I.

I took a deep breath. Exhaled. Found my voice again. Tried to sound calm. "But our Nevada custody agreement says I can live with my son anywhere in the country."

"The child's father has filed for custody in California, and unless you return immediately custody will be awarded to him." The police officer paused. "You need to come back and work this out as soon as possible. Now."

"But, but—" I stammered.

"You really don't have any time to waste."

"Okay," I said, and looked across the booth at my son. "We'll be there in forty-eight hours." I clicked off the call and laid my cell phone carefully onto the table. I sat there, very still, my palms open on my lap.

"Did we get the apartment?" Mikey bounced in his seat. "I bet we got it!"

His dark blue eyes were bright with anticipation.

I didn't say anything. I couldn't say anything. What could I possibly say? I willed the tears forming at the corners of my eyes to stay put.

"Mom?" Mikey regarded me with caution. He knew the impending signs of a crying fugue when he saw them. "Did we get the apartment?"

I looked down at lunch on the table. My half-eaten sandwich swam before me.

"Mom?" His voice was small now.

"Not exactly, honey." And with those words the tears fell.

By Labor Day, we were back in California. Our dark old basement apartment in San Tadeo long rented to someone else, we moved in with my dear friend Sandy in Cupertino. She and her husband Brian generously took in us orphans with open arms "for the duration," as Sandy put it. Sandy and I had been close since Alexis and Greg were little; she'd seen me through twenty years and two divorces. Mikey and I were in good hands.

My lawyer insisted that the situation was just temporary, that we would win in court, and be able to return to Massachusetts. It would just take time. Unfortunately, time was a four-letter word in California's overcrowded and overburdened justice system. Still, my attorney pressed for an early court date—and we were granted one within two weeks.

September 11, 2001.

Sandy was on a road trip vacation with her daughter, so my friend Susan came to see me through that unhappy day. Susan was a wonderful friend of longstanding with whom I shared many common interests; we were both writers and moms whose devotion to literature was matched only by our devotion to our kids.

We didn't watch the news before we left for court on what would become one of the most infamous days in history. So we sat in the lobby of the courthouse together, across the wide floor from my ex and Miss Priss. We tried not to watch as they held hands and whispered and watched us not watching them, all of us completely unaware of the tragedy unfolding on the other side of the country.

"You're even wearing the same shoes," Susan said to me, an unbelieving reference to the black high-heeled pumps and other many striking similarities between Miss Priss and myself.

"I like mine better," I said, knowing very well that she'd paid at least triple for hers than I'd paid for mine.

We languished there at the courthouse for what seemed like hours. I had a long time to study my look-alike nemesis, who, although far thinner than I, wore that pinched look we more voluptuous types considered characteristic of many skinny (read hungry) women. Attractive, but not the Victoria's Secret supermodel who had haunted my dreams. All that insomniac angst over nothing.

Not that I really cared. All I cared about was getting back to Massachusetts with my son before my new employer lost his patience and hired someone else to replace me. I'd already missed my first week of work. I dreaded missing a second. With any luck we'd be in and out of court today and on the road headed east tomorrow.

But this was not to be a lucky day. Everything changed on September 11, not just for me and Mikey, but for the entire planet. We were sent home from the courthouse and told to come back in five weeks. Susan took me back to Sandy's house, where we drank margaritas and watched the planes crash into the Twin Towers over and over and over again. The whole world was going crazy.

Susan stayed with me until Mikey came home from school. I called my new employer in Massachusetts, a native New Yorker reeling from the day's momentous events.

"Take whatever time you need," my boss told me, earning my heartfelt gratitude forever.

My lawyer informed me that the one with the most paperwork wins, and instructed me to get busy building my case for custody. Anyone who's ever been involved in a custody battle knows that it can get real mean, real fast. The past eighteen months had been so brutal in so many ways; I should have been prepared for this latest wretched turn of events. But I was not. I was in mourning—for me and Mikey, for my fellow Americans, for life as we had known it before this day.

I had a lot to do to prepare for court—but I was having trouble doing it. I was paralyzed by the fear, the shock, the very injustice of it all. Sandy came home from her trip and found me nearly undone. She called my parents, who drove up from Las Vegas to snap me out of it.

"I just can't believe this is happening," I told my father. We were sitting in Sandy's den, Dad in Brian's recliner, I on the couch, a crochet needle in my hand, yards and yards of blue wool on my lap. Crocheting gave my hands something to do while the rest of me panicked.

I was scared. Scared of losing my job in Massachusetts, scared of not being able to find a job in California if it came to that, scared of being unemployed and losing Mikey because of it. My ex and Miss Priss had good jobs, a big house, a whole family. I had only the slim promise of a job, no place of my own, no intact family unit.

"It *is* happening," my father said.

"But *I* have custody," I said. "I *have* custody. I have *custody.*"

I did have custody, according to our Nevada divorce agreement, but my ex had used a technicality to challenge that agreement here. Now, right or wrong, the state of California was claiming jurisdiction, and could choose—or not—to honor the Nevada agreement.

My dad pulled himself out of the recliner, and came to sit next to me on the couch. "That doesn't matter anymore."

"It's not fair," I said.

The Colonel chastened me with a harsh look I knew very well. A look reserved for pathetic morons who uttered incredibly stupid statements.

"Life is not fair," we said together at the same time, pronouncing yet another one of *The Colonel's Rules of Life.*

"And only a fool expects it to be," said my father gently, adding the all-important *Colonel's Codicil for* my benefit. As if I'd forgotten it. Which apparently I had.

"I don't want to do this," I said. "I shouldn't have to do this. It's bad for Mikey, it's bad for me, it's—"

"You have no choice," my father said.

"It's going to get ugly," I said.

"It's already gotten ugly." The Colonel placed his hands on my shoulders, squaring them for me.

I bowed my head. The crochet needle slipped from my fingers, disappearing into the folds of fuzzy blue wool.

Dad cupped his hand under my chin and lifted it up so that I could face him. "Look at me."

I looked him in the eye, knowing I wasn't going to like what he was going to tell me to do, and knowing I was going to have to do whatever it was he told me to do whether I liked it or not.

"You didn't start this fight," Dad began. "But there's no getting out of it now. If you lose, you lose your son." He gave me the barest of smiles, the smile of a warrior preparing to charge. "You are at war. Fight to win."

Fight to win. I hated fighting, but as a soldier's daughter I knew that when you were actively engaged in a fight, winning was everything. You have to fight to win. Anything less is not only potentially disastrous, it's inevitably dishonorable.

So I prepared for battle as sensibly and strategically as Patton would have done. Over the next several weeks, I put together two four-inch plastic binders full of legal documents, e-mails, letters, psychologists' evaluations, and journal entries. I was a reporter, who knew how to find a story. I was a researcher, who knew how to gather information. I was a writer, who wrote down everything. Thank God I lived an examined life—because those binders, full of that examination, gave me the ammunition I needed to win in court. My ex had his wife's lawyer and his wife's money—and I had my lawyer, my dot-com bonuses, and the singular drive borne of a mother's ruthless protection of her young.

Those were rough months. Mikey was the new kid in yet another new school in California, a new school we hoped he'd be out of soon, so he could be the new kid in yet another new school in Massachusetts. While Mikey was in the classroom, I was at the courthouse, on the Internet, in Sandy's den, documenting, researching, writing. When I wasn't working on the case, I was helping Mikey with his homework, whimpering to my stalwart friends, crocheting the world's longest, bluest afghan as a thank-you gift for Sandy. I walked for miles around the perfect suburban streets of Cupertino, partly to defuse my deep agitation and partly to counteract the pounds I was putting on thanks to the endless supply of comfort food Sandy prepared to keep my strength up. *Baked Brie. Candied almonds and honey-roasted cashews. Homemade pickles. Lentil soup. Stuffed shells. The world's most elaborate tuna fish salad. Carrot cake. Brownies. Bread pudding. Chocolate chip cookies, lemon drop cookies, oatmeal raisin cookies.*

Mikey seemed to take it all in stride, as kids often do. But one night, after his weekly Wednesday night visit with his father, he asked me how long we were going to have to live at Sandy's house.

"When can we leave, Mom?" It was past bedtime and he was sitting on the twin bed in Sandy's daughter's childhood bedroom. She was grown now, and on her own. There was no question that this was a girl's room, all white wicker adorned with bright orange and pink flowers, but Mikey never complained.

"I don't know, honey, but it could be soon. I hope it will be soon." I tucked my son into the little bed. "Shall we read tonight?"

Every night we took turns reading a new chapter in a book of his choice. I read a page, and then Mikey read a page. I'd done this with all my kids; it was one of my favorite parent-child rituals. But since we'd come to Sandy's house, we hadn't read much. We both found it hard to make sense of those little black symbols on the fresh white pages on these long, terrible nights.

"No. I hate reading. I hate books."

"That's not true. You know that's not true."

Mikey rolled over, his back toward the wall and away from me. "I miss my room. I miss Isis. I miss Shakespeare."

"Me, too, honey." Isis had joined Shakespeare at my folks' house in Las Vegas until we got our own place again. If and when we got our own place again.

"I want to go home."

I sighed. *If only we had one.* "Me, too, honey."

"We aren't going to get that apartment in Manchester-by-the-Sea, are we?" asked Mikey, as if he could read my mind.

"No, I'm afraid that place is rented already." I'd checked first thing. The landlord was sympathetic, but not *that* sympathetic. I turned off the light and sat down on the bed. Gently I reached out and rubbed Mikey's forehead. "But we'll find another great place. The North Shore is full of great places. Manchester-by-the-Sea, Rockport, Salem . . . ." My voice trailed off.

"Promise?" asked Mikey, as if I could fix everything with just a word.

"Promise," I answered firmly, as if I could fix everything with just a word.

Mikey shifted under the covers, and turned so he could see me. "Will you sing me to sleep?"

"Sure," I said, willing my voice not to crack. I had sung to all of my children when they were babies, sung them to sleep as mothers all over the world have done since the beginning of time. But there always came a dark evening when the children decided they were too old for that baby stuff—and books to read replaced songs to sing. Mikey was nine years old now, and we'd made the switch to books years before.

Mikey moved over onto his stomach. I ran my fingers lightly over his bare back, tracing letters down his spine, just as I had done when he was a toddler. And I sang all the old lullabies I'd sung to him as a baby. *Summertime. Can't Help Loving That Man of Mine. My Favorite Things. Wouldn't That be Loverly. Let It Be. You've Got a Friend. As Time Goes By. Chim Chim Cheree, Smile, Amazing Grace, Imagine, Blowin' in the Wind, Starry, Starry Night, Me and Bobby McGee, Someone to Watch Over Me.*

I sang, and Mikey closed his eyes. I sang, and Mikey dozed off into a sound slumber. I sang, and I kept on singing, long after Mikey was asleep. I sang late into the night, alone with my sleeping child in the deep gloom, my heart full of unshed tears.

My lawyer was correct. The one with the most paperwork always wins. Two months and $30,000 later, under the aegis of the Great State of California and at the urging of an enlightened guardian *ad litem*, my ex and I came to terms very similar to those terms outlined in our original Nevada agreement. Mikey and I were free to relocate to Massachusetts. Mikey would visit his father on all holidays and most of summer vacation.

"Don't set foot in this state again until he's eighteen," was the last thing my lawyer said to me before we left.

And so we escaped to New England for the third—and last—time.

chapter thirteen

"Dogs that exhibit separation anxiety often have a history that includes a 'separation event.'"

—KIMBERLY BARRY, PHD, animal behaviorist

WITH GREG LIVING WITH US AT THE COTTAGE, EVERYONE SETTLED down. Freddie and Shakespeare hung out with Greg while he wrote, the perfect canine muses. Mikey made friends, all of whom loved hanging out at the house with Greg after school. And for the first time in a long time, I had an adult at home to talk to, even though he was my own adult child. The truth is, there is nothing more gratifying than raising kids who grow into people you enjoy being with. We watched movies and talked books and debated politics; we drank wine and read each other's writing; we jogged with the dogs through the bogs.

Greg was good company for all of us—me and Mikey and Freddie. The eighteen months he spent with us was a happy time for us all. We flourished—Greg included—and we missed him when he moved out. All the writing he'd done while he was living with us paid off: Greg got a job offer out in Los Angeles to serve as editor of a financial magazine, and he took it.

It was time for him to go—Greg wasn't meant to sleep on our couch forever. Before he left, my philosophy major asked me one of those questions that often stop us parents cold. Because the answers we give in return are so important.

"How do you be happy, Mom?" Greg sat in front of the little built-in desk to the left of the oven in the kitchen, where we'd set up the desktop computer for him. He'd written two books on it, and was now contracted for a third. "How does a person find happiness?"

I stood in the middle of my kitchen, a ladle in my hand. I was making my award-winning chili, one of Greg's favorite dishes. Freddie was curled up at his feet, his gaze on the ladle, while Shakespeare had taken up his usual sentry post at the front door. "That's a very profound inquiry."

"I'm serious, Mom." Greg leaned toward me with a characteristic intensity, his deep blue eyes searching mine.

"I can see that." I stirred a tablespoon of chili powder into the spicy meat and bean soup, buying myself some time to think of the most correct and appropriate response. I decided on telling the truth as I knew it, however pretentious and portentous it may sound to my twenty-six-year-old son. "I think that to be happy in the deepest sense . . . ." My voice trailed off. I stirred vigorously, then stopped short. "I mean, happy as opposed to content." I glanced at Greg.

"Happy as opposed to content, yeah, I get it, Mom. Go on."

"To be truly happy, I think you have to figure out what it means to lead a meaningful life." I paused. "For *you*."

"A meaningful life." Greg thought about that. "How do you that? How did *you* do that?"

I grinned. "It was easy for me. I had Alexis at twenty-one, you at twenty-three. You were my *raison d'etre*. I didn't even have to think about it."

"Not everybody has kids."

"No, and even if they do, they don't usually have them that young." I placed the lid on the pot of chili and turned to face my son. "Thanks to you kids, I always had a reason to get up in the morning."

"You also had your work."

"Absolutely. I love my work. I love my kids." I shrugged.

"Love and work," said Greg. "Just like Freud said."

I laughed. "Well, that's *one* thing he got right."

Greg laughed too, then shot me a sober look. "Do you think I'll figure it out, Mom?"

"Figuring it out is what you're supposed to spend your twenties doing. You're right on schedule." I kept on stirring. "But you know, when you and Alexis were little and I was a stay-at-home mom, I was perfectly happy. I loved raising you kids. When I ended up divorced and broke, I went to work to feed you. It was only a means to an end." I tapped the ladle on the side of the pot. "But I liked it. Eventually I became ambitious for my own sake—and not simply for my family's sake."

I put down the ladle and gave him a quick hug. "A meaningful life means different things to different people. You are exploring your options."

"Alexis seems to have it all figured out," said Greg, comparing himself to his older sister unfavorably, as he'd been doing since the day he was born. "Living in Europe, singing and writing and—"

"Alexis was born knowing who she is and what she wants. Most of us aren't like that." I hugged him again, then stepped back and searched his face, hands on my hips.

"You are right on track. Look how much you've accomplished already. You've got a college degree, you've traveled abroad, you've written several books, and you've just landed your first staff position. You should be very proud of yourself."

"I guess."

"Give yourself some credit, sweetie." I went back to the stove, and lifted the lid off the chili pot. The tantalizing smell of peppery beef filled the room. Freddie jumped up, and scampered around my ankles. Shakespeare lumbered to his feet, and over to me. He cocked his head and his Beatles bangs fell to one side.

"Suppertime!" I said with a jazzy inflection. I picked out a few choice bits of meat and held them out for the dogs.

Freddie's spotted tail wagged furiously, a blur of brown and white and black.

"Food," I said to Greg. "Now that's what a meaningful life is really all about. Just ask Freddie."

That night Shakespeare and I went down to the lake before we went to bed, as we often did. Mikey and Freddie were already tucked into bed; Greg was snoring on the couch. It was late, and the stars shone brightly against the midnight sky. A rosy ring glowed around the moon—an illuminated portent of snow to come. The temperature was falling, but I was warm enough in my flannel pajamas, over which I'd thrown my woolen winter coat. I wore my insulated bog boots, and cupped a small tumbler of red wine in my gloved hands. I sat on the steps leading down to the dock, and Shakespeare settled at my feet.

"It's going to snow," I told Shakespeare. He didn't answer, but laid his bushy black head on the toe of my boot, tolerant as always of my nocturnal ruminations.

Brave words I'd blessed my son Greg with earlier. All that wise talk about *raison d'etre* and leading a meaningful life. What I'd said was true: kids and career had been my salvation. But work only took you so far—and my children were leaving one by one. Alexis had long ago flown the nest, Greg was winging his way West very shortly, and Mikey was a teenager already intent on test flights.

I was going to need a new *raison d'etre*—and soon.

Before Greg left, everyone came to the cottage for Christmas. Mikey, Greg, me, Alexis home from Europe, Mom and the Colonel in from Las Vegas, Shakespeare and Isis and Freddie. The cottage was buried in snow and love and laughter. But as the kids began to leave—Mikey for San Tadeo to spend the rest of the holiday with his father, Alexis back to her happy life in Switzerland, Greg off to his new job in Los Angeles—my mood grew more melancholy. As it inevitably did when

I realized that once again I'd be kissing my mother at midnight on New Year's Eve. Not that there's anything wrong with that.

The little village of Lytton is not exactly a party kind of town. The fact that it was snowing again made it all the easier for my parents and me to decide to ring in the New Year at home, as we usually did. Dad was watching college ball on television, switching between games on the various channels, oblivious to the woes of the women around him.

But my mother, sensing another one of my annual pity parties on the way, apparently had a plan. She pointed to the kitchen.

"Let's go teach you how to make a decent meringue." Over the years, Mom had managed to teach me how to make a good flaky pie crust, a splendid buttermilk chocolate cake, and her to-die-for fudge. But I'd always resisted the meringue, if only because I so preferred that fudge.

"Sure." I had no real interest in making meringue, now or ever, but I could tell by the way her dark brown eyes flashed with a missionary zeal that there was no stopping her now.

The dogs jumped up, alert to every nuance of my parents' behavior. Whenever my parents were here, my father spent most of his time outside on the dock sharing the secrets of good fishing with the boys or watching sports inside with the boys, and my mother spent most of hers baking countless pies, cakes, and cookies for our sweet-starved household. This visit was no exception—and it drove the dogs crazy with indecision. The excellent company of the Colonel, the world's coolest pack leader—or the sweet confections of the Colonel's wife, the world's best baker?

The dogs knew a good cook when they smelled one. As long as Mom stayed out of the kitchen, the dogs lay content at my father's feet. But the minute my mother got that sugary gleam in her eye, the dogs abandoned the Colonel. I joined Freddie and Shakespeare in Mom's wake as she headed to the kitchen to teach me the culinary intricacies of making meringue.

Marriage. Motherhood. Meringue. Otherwise known as The Sweetest Things in a Woman's Life. At least to my mother, who'd spent most of her life perfecting the art of this holy triumvirate. And the rest of it bemoaning my failure to master any of it.

It started with marriage. My mother came from the Fifties School of Life, which taught that finding the right mate was the most important decision a woman could make in her life. My mother married my father in 1954. They'd been as happy as clams ever since.

Naturally, I got it all wrong. Twice.

"We never really had any trouble until you started getting married," my mother said as she rummaged around in my kitchen, up to her elbows in eggs and sugar and baking utensils that get used once a year or whenever my mother visited, whichever came first. "That's not true." I watched as she separated the egg whites with the spare efficiency of a swordsman. "That can't possibly be true."

She ignored me as she slipped the bowl of egg whites into the microwave. Freddie and Shakespeare lay by the front door across the room, waiting for the scent of that blessed chemical reaction that would change raw eggs into doggy candy.

"The trick to a good meringue foam is temperature. The egg whites must be at room temperature—not too hot or too cold—before you beat them. If you take the eggs right out of the fridge, you'll need to warm them up a bit first."

Mom had to be wrong. There must have been *something* that caused more trouble for my folks than my unfortunate marital alliances.

"What about the war in Vietnam?" I smiled, triumphant. Dad spent a tour over there during some of the fiercest fighting of the conflict. A lot of sleepless nights for us all until he came back home safe and sound. "Now *that* was trouble. *Big* trouble."

"It didn't last as long," she said without missing a beat as she pulled the bowl out of the beeping microwave and placed it on the counter.

She had me there. I sighed. "I guess not."

Armed now with a wire whisk I didn't know I owned, my mother whipped the egg whites with a surprisingly strong seventy-year-old arm.

"Look, Mom, I didn't *mean* to cause you and Dad any trouble." I watched as the egg whites doubled and redoubled under her capable strokes in mounting folds of rich goo.

"Well, of course you didn't!" Mom whipped harder. "It wasn't *your* fault!" She whipped furiously now, agitated, and the egg whites stood at full attention in tall peaks rising out of the bowl. Freddie's ears went up on alert.

"*You* were never any trouble." She added the sugar and whipped again, attacking the foam. "It was those . . . those . . . those *husbands* of yours."

Overcome, my mother stopped short. The whisk in her hand slipped and sloppy tufts of meringue soared through the air, landing mostly on my cheeks and chin. Freddie jumped up and darted across the floor, looking for stray slops. Shakespeare followed as quickly as his aging hips allowed.

My mother stared at me. "Oh, honey, I'm so sorry!"

I laughed. "Look who's trouble now, Mom."

Mom laughed, too, once she was satisfied that she hadn't blinded me with the makings of her favorite dessert. She put the whisk down on the counter and dabbed at my face with the wet end of a dishtowel.

"I'm fine, Mom." I laughed again. "Back to the meringues."

"Of course. Before the foam falls." Mom rushed back to the bowl and spooned the meringue onto the cookie sheet in perfectly formed swirling dollops of spun-sugared bliss. Freddie and Shakespeare stood at her elbow, alert to the possibility of a liquid crumb—or better yet, a handout.

"Were they really so bad?" I answered my own question. "Yeah, I guess they were."

"They were *intense.*" My mother gave me one of her trademark *I love you but don't understand you* looks. "You've always fallen for intense men. Not good for the long haul."

I thought about this while I dipped my finger in the bowl and licked up the leftover foam. "That's true. I never really thought about it that way."

"I would have killed them both," my mother said with such force that it occurred to me that she might be a little intense herself.

"It's okay, Mom. The kids are great. I mean they're not perfect, but—"

"My grandchildren are wonderful. But that has nothing to do with their fathers."

My mother took pity on her canine fans and pitched a couple of spoonfuls of meringue into their food bowls, each in equal measure.

"What matters is that they turned out fine, Mom. The rest is ancient history."

"No, it's not. You raised those kids all on your own." Mom shook her head as she preheated the oven to 250 degrees. "And you're still doing it. You're still doing everything on your own."

In Mom's world, men were men and women did not do anything on their own, except shop. Their men paid the bills, disciplined the children, and changed the oil in the car every 3,000 miles. The women kept perfect homes, raised perfect children, and made perfect meringues. If they worked outside the home, it was because they wanted to—not because the bank had foreclosed on the house.

"Maybe I'm supposed to, Mom. Maybe my lesson this lifetime is to figure out how to do things on my own."

"Hmmph!" Mom rolled her eyes at me. "Oh, please!"

I didn't know what annoyed her more, the fact that I could believe such a thing or the New Age psychobabble I used to express it. I'm sure it was a tossup.

She slapped the rest of the meringues into place on the cookie sheet and popped it into the oven. "A woman needs a man around—just like a man needs a woman."

Mom slammed the door shut—and I shuddered on behalf of the unbaked meringues inside.

"But I thought you were against my marrying again, Mom."

"Who said anything about getting married?" My mother's voice hit a dangerously high pitch. "I'm just talking about a man here. If you could just meet the right one. . . ."

"A nonintense man?" I teased her at my own risk.

"Yes." My mother raised one of her perfect eyebrows. "A non-intense man. Like Joel."

Joel, the man my parents loved. Dad loved him because he'd served in the Navy; Mom loved him because he fixed things for me. Joel was the man my parents thought I should have married—but didn't.

"We're just friends, now, Mom, you know that."

"No man lays a woman's bathroom floor unless he's in love with her." Mom set the oven timer for an hour.

"But we're just friends, Mom. Really." I looked over at Freddie and Shakespeare, the older dog waiting patiently while his younger counterpart whimpered softly for another dollop of meringue. I scraped more leftover meringue into the dogs' bowls while Freddie tried to lick the spoon. "He helps me out with the house, I help him out with shopping for his daughter Rachel. That's all. I've accepted that, and you should, too." I paused. "Besides, I'm dating again now."

"No more of those horrible online people, I hope," my mother said in an oblique reference to Thurber.

"I met Joel online, too, Mom."

"That was years ago. Before the Internet went crazy."

"The Internet has always been crazy, Mom." I smiled, remembering when Mom used Web TV. Now she had a real computer and could download photos and log onto Skype faster than any other grandmother in Las Vegas. "No, Mom, these are real people. I'm into meeting people organically now. You know, through work, and—"

"Well, in that case . . . ." She pointed to the sink. "You wash, I'll dry."

This was family code for I have something to say and you're going to listen. We washed up; Mom talked—and I listened. Even the dogs listened.

"A good relationship is like a good meringue," she said. "None of this intense, crazy love stuff that burns out in a flash. You need to start at room temperature and warm up as you go. You set the oven on low, and over a slow heat the meringue sets."

"That's lovely, Mom." I grinned at her. "But I never did learn to make a decent meringue."

"You had your first lesson today. I hope you were paying attention."

Dishes done, Mom threw the towel at me to dry my hands. "Mikey will be going off on his own soon. You can't just waste away here with the dogs once he's gone."

"Uh, I won't be exactly wasting away, Mom. I have a job, friends, a full life that—"

"I took the liberty of inviting Joel over for dinner. He should be here in an hour."

"I see. Just about the time the meringues are coming out of the oven." My mother was nothing if not subtle.

"Exactly."

"He'll never come, Mom." I'd tried this tack before—san meringues. "He only comes during daylight hours when there's something to fix. And never on major holidays."

My mother gave me a quick hug. "There's not a man alive who can resist a good meringue."

Any more than I could resist my mother. I deposited a final swirl of meringue goo in each of the dogs' bowls, and followed my mother back to the living room. I knew that despite Mom's hopes, she was wrong about Joel. There was no convincing him to trust me with his heart again. We were friends, and that was that. Bathroom floor or no bathroom floor.

Joel called ten minutes later to say that he wouldn't be able to make it, after all.

"It *is* snowing pretty hard now," my mother said. "Maybe next time."

So it was Dad and Mom and I and the cat and the dogs that snowy New Year's Eve, after all, just as I knew it would be. The Colonel was asleep on the couch by the time the clock struck twelve. We didn't wake him.

When I kissed my mother as the ball fell on Times Square, I made a New Year's resolution. Mom was right about my not wasting away here at the cottage with the dogs. One way or another, I vowed to find myself a husband as soon as possible.

Er, *man.* Preferably one who liked beagles.

By the time Mikey got back from visiting his father after New Year's, everyone was gone—including Greg. We all missed Greg terribly—especially Freddie, with whom he shared a special bond, not to mention a propensity for mischief.

Mikey missed his big brother, too, but by now he'd made some good friends and was looking forward to starting high school in the fall. And, of course, I missed Greg as well, but I had my work and Mikey to keep me occupied.

Freddie, on the other hand, seemed to suffer an existential crisis when Greg moved out. With Greg gone, Freddie was alone in the house every weekday with Shakespeare and Isis until Mikey came home from school. The lively little beagle didn't like it—and over the next few months he made his displeasure very clear. He destroyed more shoes and cabinets and books. He peed and pooped on the hardwood floors I'd just had refinished. He howled more. He barked more and growled more and lunged at people more. Especially the men. He snapped at our neighbor Steve and our plumber Sal and every deliveryman who came to the door.

When Mikey left to spend the summer with his father, I was left alone to deal with Freddie. I moved him and Shakespeare into my two-car garage during the day while I was at work to save my house—but the stubborn hound howled all the louder and ate everything I'd put there in storage. I took him to obedience class—but he did not play nicely with others and was asked to leave. I tried using Ggentle Leader collars, choke collars, and muzzles—but he still snapped at every man and dog we passed on our walks through the bogs. I used every trick, tip, and technique in the dog-training books, to no avail.

By midsummer I was nearly out of options and nearly out of my mind. Shakespeare, heretofore the world's best dog, was picking up some of Freddie's bad habits. He became as territorial as Freddie; he even adopted Freddie's aggressive posture, charging and nipping at strangers.

I was surrounded by badly behaved animals—and I didn't know what to do about it. Every night we all piled into my postage-stamp bedroom, me and Isis on the bed, Freddie and Shakespeare on the floor beside us. Freddie was used to sleeping on Mikey's bed, and every night he tried to join me and the cat under the covers. And every night Isis showed the upstart beagle who really ruled the cottage, hissing and scratching and mewling until Freddie cowered on the floor where Isis insisted he belonged. I didn't get much sleep that summer.

The little lake house was always a lonely if lovely place for me in the summertime. The summer before had been the sweetest anomaly; I'd been so spoiled when I had Greg for company during the sunniest season on the lake. We'd spent many a warm evening out on the porch, drinking wine and watching the sun set and the moon rise and talking long into the night about politics, philosophy, and the true nature of Art. Now it was just me on the porch, the dogs at my feet and Isis on my lap. Serene, but achingly solitary.

One humid evening in late August I came home after a short business trip to find Isis missing. Per our usual routine, I'd boarded the dogs overnight, and picked them up at the kennel and brought them home. This usually prompted the return of our fearless Isis, who had the run of the cottage and lake while we were gone. I paid one of Mikey's friends to drop by and make sure she had food and water and a little attention.

Isis didn't need much attention; like most cats she was perfectly capable of taking care of herself. When loose in the great outdoors, the eight-pound tiger tabby was a ferocious hunter; over the years Isis brought home all manner of prey—mice, birds, lizards, frogs, chipmunks, and even the occasional snake. But once indoors, our intrepid predator would transmogrify into the most solicitous of lap cats, curling up on my knees when I settled down on the couch to watch TV, and sleeping on the curve of my hip at night in my antique iron bed.

Isis possessed that unique combination of compassion and intuition found so rarely in either the animal or human world; she'd been my dearest friend and greatest source of consolation over this lonesome summer and many lonesome times over the past eleven years. She knew before I did when I was just another desolate moment away from dissolving into tears, and would abandon her adventurous excursions and come back to the house. She'd hurl herself at the screen on my bedroom window to be let in, and upon my letting her in, would vault into my arms, rubbing her sweet whiskers against my cheek, catching the tears as they slid down my face, one by one.

Usually when I came home from a business trip, Isis would make a point of showing up as the car pulled into the driveway, meowing loudly to protest my absence. But this time she did not materialize as if by black magic as I unpacked the car, or settled the dogs inside, or put the kettle on for tea. I called and called and called for her, but she did not appear to take her rightful place as Queen of the Cottage.

Over the course of the evening, I took the dogs outside several times, as I always did. Each time I went out into the yard, crying out for Isis, but only the dark star-filled sky and a choir of crickets greeted me in return. I fell asleep on the couch, still listening for her plaintive meow.

I woke up around two in the morning, cramped from dozing on the sofa, and took the dogs out for one last bathroom run before going to bed. Freddie did his business quickly and pulled on the leash to go back inside. The little beagle was obviously ready for bed. But Shakespeare, loose as usual, ran to the edge of the yard, barking and barking. Intrigued, Freddie bounded forward, dragging me along behind him, joining his older canine companion in the yowling.

"Come on, guys," I said.

But the old dog stood his ground and his young sidekick Freddie stayed with him. I couldn't see anything, couldn't hear anything.

"Come on," I said again, and tugged at Freddie's lead. Freddie relented, and trotted after me. But Shakespeare refused to budge. In fact, he moved closer to the road, his baritone bark deepening with every step.

"Shakespeare!" I let Freddie into the house and then came back outside alone. "What is the matter with you?"

I joined Shakespeare in the middle of the road and tried to figure out exactly what my habitually mellow mutt was so worked up about. He was obviously barking at something, but I couldn't tell what. I peered into the impenetrable summer's eve gloom.

And then I saw it, a small dark something along the edge of the road by the tree line. I stepped forward. The small dark something moved, just barely. And mewed, just barely.

"Isis?" I ran across the street. There was our sweet kitty, in a low crouch, shaking, and wheezing. She was not herself. I picked the limp little feline up and quickly carried her into the house, Shakespeare on my heels. I cradled the weak, ill cat in my arms, cooing her name over and over again. "Isis, baby, what's wrong? Isis."

Her breathing labored, her eyes closed, she trembled at my touch. As I stroked her matted fur, clumps of it fell out. Convulsing now, Isis coughed violently—and then was silent. She opened her gold-green eyes, and looked right through me, then closed them once again and seemed to fall asleep. There was no saving her; somehow I knew she was going to die right there in my arms. All I could do was hold her.

Her breathing grew shallower and shallower, and within minutes she was gone. I sat dry-eyed there in the dark, Shakespeare's big shaggy head on my knee right by Isis's side, and held her lifeless body on my lap for a long, long time.

I didn't cry for Isis then, or in the hot summer days that followed. I worked, and I came home to the cottage. I fed the dogs, and walked them through the bogs. I watched stupid sitcoms and sappy movies and sat down by the water with Shakespeare and Freddie under the stars, drinking red wine and feeling sorry for myself. But I, the champion crier, did not cry.

Weeks later, not long before Mikey was due home, a big storm hit the South Shore. The wind tore around the little cottage; torrents of rain pounded the roof. Choppy waves formed white caps on the lake. I stood out on the screened porch with the dogs, only somewhat protected from the driving rain. Lightning flashed, brightening the great pond. Thunder boomed, and the dogs thundered in return.

The tempest raged all around me. Sheets of rain pelted the porch, penetrating the screens and smattering me with warm gushes of wet mist. The tears, too, came in a rush. While Freddie and Shakespeare howled along with the wind, I cried for the dear cat who'd brightened our lives for eleven years. I cried for Mikey, stuck at Miss Priss's house for yet another summer. And I cried for myself, alone on a hot stormy August night on the pond, with no one for company but two increasingly badly behaved dogs.

chapter fourteen

"Dogs want to know what to do with their lives. Let the dog work for your affection."

—CESAR MILLAN

THAT INTERMINABLE, MISERABLE SUMMER FINALLY CAME TO AN END AS all summers inevitably do. Mikey came home from California, and started his first year of high school. He joined the freshman football team, and spent long hours on the playing field. I drove him back and forth to practice, attended all his games, and helped flip burgers at the snack bar with the other football parents. Freddie and Shakespeare stayed home, no longer fit to attend children's sporting events.

In October my parents came to visit, a visit ostensibly planned around the Northeast's splendid fall foliage and Mikey's football games. The Colonel was thrilled that his grandson was playing his favorite sport (well, at least one of his favorite sports). And my mother had always wanted to experience autumn in New England.

First came the foliage. The trees that lined the lake were just beginning to turn, so we took off for Maine in search of brightly colored leaves. We drove and drove, but we never did find any leaves. Apparently autumn was late this year. So the trip should not be a total loss, we headed for the coast on the way home, and stopped at the Maine Diner in Wells for the tourist trap's justifiably famous lobster rolls and blueberry pie.

"This is the best meal we ever had in New England," the Colonel said, dismissing every four-star restaurant I'd treated him to over the past several years with a wave of his plastic lobster bib.

"I'm glad you like it." I smiled, thinking of all the money I'd save in the future, now that Dad had discovered the one-of-a-kind Maine Diner.

Back home at the cottage on the lake, we prepared for the big game. I was worried that it might prove as disappointing for my folks as the fall foliage had. Mikey was a second string defensive end. The coach never played the second string—even though his precious first string had yet to win a game. I'd sent the stubborn man an e-mail before the game, basically begging the guy to let Mikey spend some time on the field for his grandparents' sake. He never answered me.

At least the weather was good. It was one of those perfect sunny, crisp early October days which begged for sweaters and apple cider and football under a bright, blue sky. We sat in the bleachers, me and Mom and the Colonel, with all of the other freshman football parents.

"It's so nice to have you and Dad here, Mom."

Mom patted my hand. "Well, it's nice to be here."

"Usually I have to come to these games by myself." I tossed my head at the other parents, all couples who came in twos as if they were lining up for Noah's ark. "I'm always the only single parent here. It's . . . depressing."

"Uh huh."

"Seriously, Mom, this state has the lowest divorce rate in the union." I lowered my voice so all the married couples around me wouldn't hear. "Even the people who do get divorced marry again quickly so as not to offend the locals. I'm a pariah here."

"What about Joel?"

Not Joel, again? I thought. *The woman was like Freddie with a bone.* "We're just friends, Mom."

"Uh huh."

"Really, Mom."

"If you say so." My mother smiled. "Well, you'll find someone soon."

"I don't know, Mom. At my age there aren't that many fish left in the sea."

"There will always be somebody for someone like you, no matter how old you are. You're just like your Grandma Emma. And she was married *three* times. That last time in her sixties."

Thank the Lord for my paternal grandmother, the only one in our entire extended family who'd been married more times than I had. A charming small-town Indiana girl with a winning personality who drew men like bees to her famous homemade honey butter. When she died, we found engagement rings from men we never even knew she'd liked, and certainly never married. She was my family heroine.

The call of his mother's name prompted my father to participate in this conversation, the sort he'd usually leave to my resourceful mother. "Just because there are fewer fish in the sea, doesn't mean you should settle for carp."

"Excuse me?"

"Carp. Bottom feeders." Dad cleared his throat. "Hold out for trout."

"Trout?" I asked, hoping for a little clarification.

But my father, having contributed all he had to offer in this domestic exchange, turned his attention back to the field, leaving my mother to follow up.

"Your father's right," said Mom. "You need to hold out for trout. I'm sure you'll catch one soon. I *know* you will."

"Yeah." I laughed. "You and St. Jude."

St. Jude was the saint of lost causes, my mother's favorite saint.

"I don't know what you're talking about."

"Come on, Mom. I know about that deal you made with God."

My mother stiffened. "I did no such thing."

"Mom, you stopped going to Mass years ago."

"I always watched it on TV."

"But ever since California," I continued, "you've gone to church every Sunday."

By unspoken agreement, we always referred to the terrible time of the custody battle as "California," the Golden State tarnished forever in our collective family memory.

"There's nothing wrong with going to church every Sunday. You're supposed to go to church every Sunday."

I put my arm around her shoulder. "I know, Mom. But you started going again then, and you're still going now."

"I'm thankful, that's all." My mother looked at me, her eyebrows raised in righteousness. "I'm thankful you got through all that. And now that you have, I'm thankful for the man you're going to meet."

"Me, too. I'm sure St. Jude won't let us down."

"Just don't marry him," my mother said.

I laughed. "Jeez, Mom," I teased, "I'm not sure St. Jude would approve of that."

Naturally Mom didn't think that was at all funny. She cocked her head and raised those magnificent eyebrows at me. "Oh, okay," she said with a faint growl, "if you must marry him, I have two words for you: Pre. Nup."

"The game is starting." The Colonel changed the subject for us, and we abandoned all talk of saints and fish to concentrate on Mikey's football game.

For the first three quarters of the game, Mikey sat on the bench, just as he had most every game thus far. The lopsided score—seventeen to nothing—was not in our side's favor. It never was.

As the contest wore on, and Mikey sat on the bench with the other second-stringers, I grew more and more agitated. The other parents were grumbling, too. The coach rubbed us moms and dads the wrong way, and had from the start, thanks to this infuriating pattern of playing only the first-stringers every game, even though they weren't any better than the second-stringers, much less good enough to win a game. This stubborn losing strategy irritated us all, players and parents alike, to the point of distraction, game after game.

But my parents had come 2,000 miles and I was determined that they were going to see Mikey on the field in the game if I had to sell my soul to make it happen. I hopped off the bleachers and made my way down to the sidelines. I took up my glaring post, and stared at the hapless coach. At one point, he turned to yell at the water boy and caught my eye. If looks could kill, he'd be as dead as an offside play.

Just as the game counted down the last five minutes of the fourth quarter, just as I perfected my death glare, just as I was ready to abandon the death glare and simply throttle that coach with my bare bejeweled hands, he sent Mikey out to play. Our handsome defensive end trotted out to the field and took his place at the end of the defensive line, accompanied by significant whooping on the part of his mother and grandmother. Mom and I held our breath as the ball went into play and the players surged forward; the Colonel placed his hands on his knees and leaned in, eyes on his youngest grandchild.

Mikey threw the tight end out of the way, tackled the running back, and disappeared in a melee of arms and legs and helmets. The Colonel smiled, actually showing teeth, while Mom and I whooped some more. On the next play, Mikey was back on the bench while the offense went to work.

But the offense stumbled. A bad pass led to an interception. The other team got the ball and kept it, and Mikey's team went on to lose the game, just as they'd lost all the others.

Still, Mikey had his brief shining moment in the October sun, so we were all happy as we celebrated Mikey's victorious tackle back at the cottage with a picnic on the porch. On the menu, Mikey's favorite meal: my mother's chicken casserole, followed by her homemade cheesecake and Rice Krispy Treats. I made the salad. Mom doesn't make salad.

After supper, our neighbor Steve dropped by to say hello, and both Freddie and Shakespeare barreled to the front door, barking and growling and lunging. When the Colonel told Shakespeare to back off, he did. But Freddie was all aggression and attitude; he ignored the Colonel, and continued to bark and growl and pull on the leash we kept on him round the clock these days. Finally, I instructed Mikey to put Freddie in the garage for the duration of Steve's visit. My parents were horrified; they couldn't believe that the adorable puppy they'd met two years before had morphed into the howling demon dog from hell.

After Steve left, Mikey brought Freddie back into the house and they disappeared into his room. That's when Dad took me aside. We went down to the water, and sat at the picnic table, watching the moon rise over the lake.

"You've got to do something about that dog," the Colonel said.

"I don't know what else I can do, Dad. We've tried everything."

"You need to *train* him." Training dogs came as easy to the Colonel as training soldiers.

But not to me. "I've tried, Dad. I took him to that obedience class, but he wouldn't settle down. He kept barking at the other dogs. They told me he wasn't ready." I sighed. "And I've tried training him myself, but all I can get him to do is sit. And then only if I give him popcorn as a reward."

"Popcorn." Dad frowned. "You don't train a dog with popcorn."

"Let's face it, Dad. I'm no better with dogs than I am with husbands."

"You have to start out with a trainable husband."

"Trout." I smiled.

"You can't train a fish," Dad said impatiently. "This is not about fish."

"I see," I said, although clearly I didn't. I was having trouble keeping up with my father's animal metaphors.

"What you need is a Golden Retriever."

"A Golden Retriever?" I was truly lost in Dad's dogspeak now.

"Kind, loyal, protective, good-natured." Dad paused. "Trainable."

"So I didn't marry Golden Retrievers. I married . . . ." I struggled to come up with the right, er, wrong breed.

"Dobermans."

"Dobermans," I repeated.

"You married Dobermans." The Colonel leaned back and placed his hands on his knees. "When I was a boy, we had a neighbor with a pair of Dobermans. Old Mrs. Schmidt." He leaned toward me. "She loved those dogs. Babied them. And they loved her back." Dad lifted his arms and opened his palms. "Until the day they tore her apart."

"Oh my God," I said. "Poor Old Mrs. Schmidt."

"Yep." Dad nodded. "Never trust a Doberman. They'll turn on you when you least expect it."

"Never marry a Doberman." I got it now. "They'll turn on you when you least expect it."

"What you need is a Golden Retriever," the Colonel said. "Like Joel."

"Okay," I said. "So my ex-husbands are Dobermans and Joel is a Golden Retriever." I took a deep breath and asked the question I didn't want my father to answer. "What does that make me, Dad? Some high-strung French poodle in high heels?" I giggled, as much out of angst as humor.

The Colonel stared at me. "Absolutely not. You're some goddamn Saint Bernard always racing out into a blizzard to rescue some yahoo who doesn't deserve rescuing."

I didn't know what to say to that. Most of my exes—husbands and boyfriends alike—were rescue projects in one way or another. But I didn't really want to rehash all of my romantic mistakes with the Colonel yet again. So I changed the subject.

"What about beagles?" I looked at Dad.

"My Trixie was a beagle and she was a good dog. But she was only part beagle."

"Other people train beagles. They train them to sniff out drugs at airports and find termites in houses and detect disease in crops."

Dad gave me a questioning look.

"Mikey and I looked it up when we first got the dog." I sighed. "So is Freddie a trainable dog? Or is it just me?"

The Colonel shrugged. "I don't know. I don't see enough of him." Dad pursed his lips. "He's a beagle." Dad shook his head. "This pure-bred beagle is trouble. And Shakespeare is adopting all his bad habits. Shakespeare may be a mutt, but he's a good dog. I'm not so sure about this one."

"I know. When it's just us, he's fine. But whenever a guy comes over, he goes berserk."

"Unacceptable," the Colonel said.

"I know," I said again. "But Mikey loves that dog, Dad." I couldn't bear to see my son suffer any more disappointment. Especially at my hands.

"I understand that," said Dad. "That's why you have to do something, before he hurts somebody and it's too late." Dad paused. "Have you had him fixed yet?"

"No." I hadn't even thought about it. We'd adopted Shakespeare and Isis; animals from the pound were always spayed and neutered as a matter of course. Not so purebred dogs.

"Get him fixed," Dad said. "That should help."

And with the Colonel's words ringing in my ears, fixing Freddie became my obsession—and a living, breathing, howling metaphor for my broken life. If I could only fix Freddie, then maybe I could fix what ailed Mikey: his relationship with his father, his teenage apathy, his own little broken heart. If I could only fix Freddie, then maybe I could fix what ailed me: my empty bank account, my empty bed, my own little broken heart.

If I could only fix Freddie, maybe I could fix my life.

Mr. Fix It: *noun*, someone adept to finding solutions to problems, household and otherwise

chapter fifteen

"The interest in roaming is eliminated in 90 percent of neutered dogs. Aggressive behavior against other male dogs is eliminated in 60 percent of neutered dogs. Urine marking is eliminated in 50 percent of neutered male dogs. Inappropriate mounting is eliminated in 70 percent of neutered dogs."

—WENDY BROOKS, DVM

O TO ANY COCKTAIL PARTY IN A SUBURBAN NEIGHBORHOOD ON THE South Shore, and after the obligatory exchanges about kids and work and landscaping, sooner or later the conversation will turn to dogs. Every self-respecting household in the Commonwealth has at least one dog, the majority of which seem to be Labs, golden retrievers, and mutts adopted through Petfinder. com—not necessarily in that order. (South Shore people are dog people: Think black Lab T-shirts, the Boston terrier, and Claire Cook, the author of *Must Love Dogs*.)

And when the subject of dogs does come up, one of the women (it's always one of the women) will ask which veterinarian you trust with your beloved canines and when you have the good sense to answer, "Dr. B," all the women will titter with pleasure and all the men will roll their eyes in disbelief.

That's because Dr. B is generally acknowledged to be the most handsome and most compassionate veterinarian in three counties. If not the world. Shakespeare and Isis always loved Dr. B, as did Freddie as a puppy. But now that Freddie had taken an unreasonable dislike to all men outside our immediate family, I was worried about taking the poorly mannered, man-hating hound back to see the good doctor.

I held Freddie tightly on the leash and approached the animal hospital carefully. I opened the door and stuck my head in, keeping Freddie at bay with my raised foot. The coast was clear: no dogs, no people in the lobby except for a blond receptionist behind the front desk and a little old lady with a cat carrier on the far side of the room. Freddie liked blondes and little old ladies, and wouldn't bother with a feline trapped in a portable kennel, as there was little fun in that. I pulled the inquisitive beagle inside, and he trotted along next to me happily. When I seated myself on the bench in the lobby across from the elderly cat lady, Freddie parked his butt next to my feet as gentlemanly as a seeing-eye dog.

But then a pumped guy with Celtic tattoos on his thick forearms came in with an alert, muscular Doberman pinscher, and Freddie jumped up, lunging and growling and howling, as if we were any match for the muscular 100-plus-pound guard dog and the bodybuilding champ he was sworn to protect. The champ and his Doberman sat on the bench directly opposite us, their four eyes intent upon me and Freddie, sizing us up in silence: one middle-aged book editor and one noisy beagle. Clearly no real threat, but a nuisance that might have to be dealt with should the current cacophony prove prolonged.

In the interest of serenity and survival, I decided to remove the source of all this potential trouble. Namely, Freddie.

"We'll just wait outside," I shouted to the receptionist over Freddie's hollering, and dragged the big-shot bawler out the door and across the parking lot to the side lawn, where every male canine patient of Dr. B's had left his mark, providing enough odiferous tantalizations to lull Freddie into a sweet if temporary silence.

"Go ahead, Freddie, sniff all you want," I said as I shuffled along behind the deliriously overstimulated hound. "Knock yourself out, but you're still getting fixed."

Ten minutes later, the receptionist came out to retrieve us. The Doberman was nowhere to be seen, and we slipped into one of the examination rooms without incident. Still, I was worried, especially given the recent ruckus with the champ and his Doberman in the lobby. How would Freddie react to the equally buff Dr. B, however charming?

"He doesn't like men anymore," I blurted out when the world's most handsome and compassionate vet stepped inside the room and shut the door behind him. Freddie charged, and I jerked him back with a tight rein on his lead.

"Beagles," said Dr. B with a smile, as if that exonerated Freddie of any and all bad behavior. The tall man slid into a graceful squat and opened his palms. "Let the leash go."

Freddie dove for the vet.

"Hi, Freddie." Dr. B let Freddie sniff him, and then befriended the belligerent beast with a simple scratch behind his ears. "So what's the problem?"

I dove into my practiced litany of Freddie complaints: barking, lunging, growling, and snapping, among other inappropriate forms of aggression. "My dad says I should get him fixed."

Dr. B turned his Paul Newman blue eyes from Freddie to me. "Well, certainly we recommend that all dogs be neutered or spayed as a matter of course. Neutered, in Freddie's case." He turned that irresistible smile on me. "Regardless of your dog's behavior."

"Yes, of course. Doing our part to control the animal population and all that." I paused. "But if we neutered him, we could reap other benefits as well, correct?"

"Neutering a male dog can help with some aggressive behaviors," Dr. B said, rubbing Freddie's silky ears. "It will lower his testosterone levels."

"That sounds wonderful!" I said, perhaps too brightly.

Dr. B cast me an odd look. "But he'll still be Freddie."

"Well, since we need to do it anyway . . . ." My voice trailed off.

"We'll schedule the procedure," Dr. B said. "And then we'll see what happens."

They say bad things happen in threes. But as a writer I know that *everything* happens in threes. Or should, if the writer wanted to maintain any sense of editorial integrity. If something happened more than once in your story, then it should happen three times—not two. Because while something may indeed happen only once in any given narrative, if it happened twice, it was bound to happen a third time.

This was the Rule of Three. Things that happened in threes were sweeter or meaner, funnier or sadder, more successful or more disastrous. Three was the most satisfying number, whether you were talking the three-act structure, the Holy Trinity, or the three wishes always granted in fairy tales.

The Rule of Three always informed my life as a mother and as a writer:

I was born into a nuclear family of three: My mother, the Colonel, and me.

My mother had three sisters. I bore three children. I hoped to have three husbands. (Just don't tell my mother.)

So while I often lamented that bad things happened in threes, I was resigned to that all-powerful prime number defining my life. When faced with a pair of things just begging to be fulfilled by a third, I was frequently compelled by some subconscious drive for whole-ness to provide the missing element in the trio before me.

I had three pets. And then Isis died. She had been my first cat, and like your first love affair, you never really get over your first cat. But sooner or later, you encountered another appealing character, and before you could say meow, you found yourself in love again.

That's how it happened with Alice. Another long, cold winter had come and gone, and Mikey and I were at the gardening center on a cool spring Saturday afternoon, stocking up on perennials and annuals. I pulled my little red wagon of petunias and pansies, violas and snowdrops, marigolds and primroses up to the little garden shed in the nursery, where the cashier waited to ring up customers. Under the potter's bench that held the cash register sat a calico cat, resplendent among pots and pots and pots of bright red geraniums. She looked up at me with that cool disinterested gaze that so endeared us to felines, and I remembered like a blow to my heart why I needed another creature in my life.

"Mikey," I said, pointing to the calico under the bench. "Look at that cat. Just sitting there, pretty as a picture. Is she adorable or what?"

Mikey looked at the cat and then he looked at me. "You want another cat, don't you, Mom?" Mikey missed Isis, too, and had on more than one occasion suggested that we adopt another kitty. But I always demurred, too attached to my first love to entertain even the thought of another.

"I want a cat," I said tentatively, testing the idea with a roll of my tongue.

"I told you we should get another one." Mikey sighed, the unearthly moan of a teenager dealing with an ungainly grownup. "It's been nearly a year since Isis died, Mom. We should get one."

"Now," I told Mikey. "Let's go get another cat *now*." I thrust my credit card at the clerk with impatience.

Sensing my agitation, she rang me up quickly, and Mikey and I sprinted off to the car with the plants. While I packed the back of our mini-SUV with flowers, Mikey got out his phone and researched all the pet adoption centers within ten miles. No more pet mills for us. I just hoped there'd be some kitties available right away.

"There are a couple of cats at the shelter in Thayerville," Mikey said.

"Great," I said. "What are their hours on Saturday?"

"They're open for another forty-five minutes."

Taking every back road shortcut we knew, we made it with fifteen minutes to spare. Housed in a small, shingled building, the Thayerville ASPCA was long on love and short on animals to adopt.

"We have two cats right now," the ASPCA lady said. "They're both lovely." She pointed into the next room, where a black short-haired male with a white face jumped from overstuffed chair to overstuffed chair, while a tiny Maine coon female curled in one corner of the smaller chair watched her companion's acrobatics with amusement.

Both cats approached us immediately, rubbing our legs and purring.

"They're friendly kitties," the ASPCA lady said, making her obligatory pitch. "And they get on so well together."

Mikey grinned. "Two cats are better than one."

"Don't even think about it," I told him. "The house is too small as it is." I turned to the ASPCA lady. "Besides, we really need to stick to female cats. We're allergic."

I picked up the little female. "How is she with dogs?"

"She's fine with other animals," said the ASPCA lady. "She came from a home with kids and dogs and cats."

"Great. We have two dogs." I stroked the kitty's long feathery tiger fur. "Our tabby Isis died about a year ago."

"I'm sorry." The ASPCA lady paused respectfully for a moment, then pounced. "She *is* cute, isn't she?"

The little Maine coon cat purred and rubbed her cheek against mine. I smiled and looked over at Mikey with a questioning glance. He nodded in agreement.

"We'll take her," Mikey said.

"Her name is Baby," the ASPCA lady told him.

Mikey wrinkled his nose. "I don't think so. We can do better than that. Right, Mom?"

This from the boy who had named every pet he ever had Freddie.

I laughed, cuddling our new little kitty. "I'm sure we'll think of something."

On the way home, Mikey held the cat carrier with our precious feline cargo on his lap. "Isis hated being in this thing. But this one doesn't seem to mind so much."

"She's pretty mellow." I tried to keep my eyes on the road. "Which is good. We've got enough trouble with Freddie. We don't need another crazy animal in the house."

"I've been thinking about a name," Mikey said. "Your favorite writer is Shakespeare, and you named Shakespeare after him. Your second favorite writer is Alice Hoffman. Why don't we call her Alice?"

There are times when even the most obnoxious of teenagers will surprise you with the same baby-powder sweetness they showered on you when they were small—and your heart stops.

"Alice," I said. "Oh honey, that's just perfect. Alice it is."

And so we took Alice home to our little cottage on the lake. Freddie and Shakespeare accepted the cheerful cat with a minimum of fuss: a few sniffs, a few howls, a few meows—and the introductions were over.

We settled down on the couch to watch television, Alice on my lap at my end of the sectional, the dogs in their little beds on the floor close to Mikey at his end of the sectional. Three pets, two people, one TV set fully equipped with more than 200 cable channels. The All-American formula for happiness in the twenty-first century.

The trouble with the Rule of Three was that once you satisfied one three-part cycle, another was bound to come along. Bad things did happen in threes. And I was right on schedule for a triple whammy of woe.

It started in Connecticut. I was invited to speak at a writer's conference there. It was September on Long Island Sound. The moon was nearly full and it shone on the water like a beacon to love and literature. There was a party for the conference staff and faculty on a boat that sultry night; we stood on the top deck under the stars as the vessel sailed out into the Atlantic and drank wine and talked about books and writing and art. A dangerous scenario for me: It had been a couple of years since Thurber, Joel and I were going nowhere but friendship (no matter what my mother thought), and my infrequent dates were frequently awful.

There was the Mainer who looked just like Santa Claus, right down to his long snowy white beard and bowlful of jelly; the geologist whose screaming ex-girlfriend showed up in the middle of our first date at the local pub, prompting a frightful scene right out of *The Jerry Springer Show*; and the gun collector who rowed me out into the Atlantic Ocean on a tandem kayak, only to inform me as soon as we were too far from shore for me to swim back on my own that he was "a pacifist who always carried a piece." Even while kayaking.

In short, I was an affair waiting to happen.

Harley was an "all hat and no cattle" cowboy journalist from Montana. He was a stocky, balding guy with the con man confidence typical of newspapermen. I'd started out as a journalist early in my career, and was a sucker for these guys. Especially the foreign correspondents. God save me from the foreign correspondents.

"I spent a year on assignment in Afghanistan," said Harley.

"Really," I said, and smiled my special smile, the one that had never yet failed to win a man.

"Would you like another glass of wine?" Harley asked.

"Sure," I said.

Five hours later we were both more than a little drunk, and more than a little in love. We spent the weekend together at the conference and then went back to our respective homes—his out West, mine back East.

That's when, separated by some 2,000 miles, our whirlwind courtship began in earnest. We were writers, and we seduced one another with words. Thousands of words a day in e-mails, phone calls, text messages.

I'd fallen in love with a writer. Again. Only this time, it was serious.

I'd been falling in love with writers since I learned to read at the age of five. Sitting on my mother's lap, I would follow her finger with my eyes as she intoned the silly syllables of Dr. Seuss, my first love. I fell hard—what girl hasn't?—for his wit, his whimsy, his wanton way with the written word. Some forty years later, I could still recite his magnum opus, *One Fish Two Fish Red Fish Blue Fish*, in its entirety, from memory. And still cry at the beauty of it.

By the time I was seven, the raucous rhymes of Dr. Seuss were no longer enough to keep my exclusive interest. There were more fish in the sea, more than I could count, right in that wonderful ocean of books called the local library. There I discovered writers who wrote books about boys and girls just like me doing fantastic things: Frank Baum and Dorothy, Donald J. Sobel and Encyclopedia Brown, E. B. White and Fern. I flirted wildly with all of these writers, but grew serious about none. For there was no *one* writer to whom I would pledge my deepest, darkest young passion. Capturing my Jungian little heart required double the literary delectability—and I found it in the Brothers Grimm. Night after night, I shined a flashlight under my covers to illuminate the gruesome, magical tales of love and loss, journey and justice, hamartia and heroism.

This love affair with the Grimm boys went on for years. But finally I grew tired of the patriarchic promises inherent in *once upon a time* and *happily ever after*. There was more to life beyond the castle walls, even for us princesses. I found myself drawn to writers who could show me what that life could be—smart, funny, compassionate women who seduced me with their daring heroines: Carolyn Keene and Nancy Drew, Louisa May Alcott and Jo, Jane Austen and Elizabeth. No more moats for me; I'd break all the rules and still meet my Mr. Right. Right? Maybe. By college the mere concept of Mr. Right seemed obsolete. As I grew into womanhood, I fell in love with women writers who celebrated being female—and all that being female could mean. Time for literary experimentation! I was flying with Erica Jong, christening the women's room with Marilyn French, exploring my secret garden with Nancy Friday. Move over, male writers: make room for the sacred feminine!

Sooner or later, the sacred feminine led to the Big M: Motherhood. Becoming a mom brought me back to literary equilibrium. I reread all my old favorites to my children, bumping into all those old loves with affection and admiration. And while my babies slept, I immersed myself in a sensual bath of muscular prose by the Johns: Cheever, Updike, Irving. I lost myself in Shakespeare, Hemingway, Fitzgerald, and all the women who wrote as men, notably George Sand and George Eliot.

Like many avid readers, I longed to learn to write myself. While my babies napped, I wrote essays, reviews, articles, short stories, even a novel. I took classes at night and joined a writer's group. Most important, I started to read as a writer, and the reading fed my writing even as the writing fueled my reading.

When my children reached school age, I went to work in publishing—first as a writer and later as an editor, beginning a career-long dalliance with more writers than I could count or even remember. As an editor and writer, my world was words and my heroes were wordsmiths. Every day brought new writers to fall for— and I fell for them on a regular basis. After more than twenty years in the business, I was still a sucker for a good writer.

And Harley was a living, breathing writer who could grace my life as well as the page. Not a crazy poet turned investment banker like my first husband. Not a wannabe James Thurber like Thurber. And not an anti-intellectual who thought all writers were crazy, like my second husband. But a real writer who loved writers, a man as silly as Dr. Seuss, as profoundly male as Hemingway, as entertaining as the Brothers Grimm. A literate cowboy as grounded in his wild places as the Johns were in theirs. It was love at first word—like reading Pablo Neruda for the first time.

I loved to read his work—and he loved to read mine. As an editor who spent her days polishing other writers' work, the writer in me had been relegated to nights for years. And after that terrible time in California, I'd found it impossible to write fiction at all. I began to think of myself as an editor first and a writer second, if at all. But falling in love with Harley reminded me that I was a writer first—and always would be. His passion and commitment to storytelling inspired me to tell my own stories again. Buoyed by his praise and encouragement, I started a new novel. The first fiction I'd written in seven years.

For the first time in a long time, I was truly happy. I was in love—with Harley, with writing, with myself. I was doing my own work, inspired by my own man. He asked me if I could consider living in Montana, once Mikey was grown—and I said yes. Of course I could live in Montana. I could live anywhere with him. I could write anywhere with him.

Harley was my once-upon-a-time come true—even if he were halfway across the country. He called me at 9 A.M. every day to say good morning; he called me every night to ask me what was for dinner, then talked to me about my day as I made supper for Mikey. He read everything I wrote—and praised it. He went to South America to visit his father, and sent me a volume of Pablo Neruda's poetry—in the original Spanish. He started applying for jobs in New England with the understanding that he would live here with us until Mikey went to college, and then we'd move West. Anything for my cowboy.

We met in New Orleans for a romantic Thanksgiving, where I introduced him to my dearest childhood girlfriends Carol and Renee, the ones who'd known me since I was fifteen, the ones who'd known every man I'd ever loved. Carol, Renee, and I were in the same class at Ursuline Academy in New Orleans, the oldest girls' school in the nation, run by the Ursuline nuns with as much charm as discipline. We'd been close ever since, even as life pulled us in different directions. Carol lived in Atlanta, Renee in New Orleans, and I was everywhere—but we still managed to get together around once a year. And whenever I met a man I thought might be the one, I made sure he met them.

Harley arranged for us to stay in a romantic bed-and-breakfast in the heart of the French Quarter, a lovely inn as charming as the Crescent City herself. We walked the cobblestone streets and drank hurricanes and made love in the four-poster bed. Renee and her husband Rob threw us a dinner party at their warm and elegant period home uptown off Saint Charles Avenue; Carol and her husband Tim drove in from Atlanta just for the occasion. Harley regaled them all with stories about his journalistic jaunts around the world, and I reveled in the thought that I'd finally found a man who could win over my dearest friends. I was happy.

Harley left early; he had to get home to the newspaper. I walked him to his car, and he slipped a smooth black stone into my pocket as he kissed me goodbye. Dizzy, I held the stone in my hand, and floated back into Renee's house.

"I like him," Renee said. "He seems, well, normal."

"Normal is good," I said.

"Normal is different," Carol said. "At least for you."

I laughed, "Yeah. I know."

"You're in love with him," Renee said, stating the obvious as she poured champagne into crystal flutes.

"Yes, I am."

"Are you going to marry him?" Carol held up her glass. "Are we toasting husband number three?"

"Maybe." I smiled, and held up the gleaming stone. "He just gave me this."

"It's a rock," Renee said.

I swooned. "Yes."

"A rock," Carol repeated.

"It's a very special rock." I paused. "In his novel, he tells the story of a goddess who leaves black stones as talismans of her affection when she falls in love with mere humans."

"Which makes you the mere human in this scenario?" Carol frowned. "You?"

"That can't be right." Renee smiled at me. "You're the goddess!"

"I certainly feel like one!" I poured us each another glass of champagne.

"I don't know," Carol said. "That's not the kind of rock a goddess like you should be getting. I think you deserve a real rock!"

"Here's to a real rock for Christmas!" Renee said.

We all laughed—and I squeezed the black rock between my fingers.

Harley and I couldn't be together for Christmas, as he had already made his plans with family out there, as I had made mine with my own family here at home. I was disappointed, of course, but what was one Christmas out of the lifetime of Christmases to come?

I knew something was up when he sent me a timepiece as a Christmas present—a crystal clock in the shape of a nineteenth-century New England schooner.

"The gift of time," he said, when he called me on Christmas Eve.

Carol would tell me that it wasn't the real rock I deserved, but I shrugged it off. Harley wouldn't be the first man whose gift-giving skills left something to be desired. You could train a man to give a good gift. My second husband was proof of that. (If only I could have trained him to like me and my kids.) And we'd already talked about meeting in Savannah in February for Valentine's Day, another prime rock-giving holiday.

I could wait for Valentine's Day for my rock, but I couldn't wait that long to see him again. So I planned a trip West for his fiftieth birthday in early January. But when I told him I'd booked the trip, he demurred. He didn't do birthdays, he said.

I knew then that something was very, very wrong. I told him on the spot that it was over. I didn't want a man who couldn't—or wouldn't—share the big moments of his life with me. You couldn't train a man to do that, even if you wanted to. My first husband was proof of that.

Desolate, I confided in Janene, a mutual friend from the writer's conference where we'd first met. I told her about my affair with Harley for the first time.

"Oh my God," Janene said. "I can't believe he would set you up like that."

"I know," I said. "I don't understand how he could be so into me, and then—"

"Do you want to know the truth?" Janene sounded uncertain.

"Uh, yeah."

"Harley has been living with another woman for, gee, at least ten years."

"What?"

"I've met her. She's nice."

"Nice?"

"I can't believe he would do this to you," Janene repeated. "Or to her."

"Ten years," I said. *How could I have missed ten years? How could he have hidden ten years?*

"They're supposed to get married next summer," Janene said. "At least that's what she told me."

Once again I'd played the fool. Once again I'd fallen for an untrainable man, a Doberman in disguise. Once again I found myself alone on New Year's Eve.

It was unseasonably warm that December; the pond was ice free. Shortly before midnight I went out on the dock and counted down to the New Year. At the last terrible stroke of twelve, I hurled that crystal clock into the lake. By the light of a nearly full moon, I watched my gift of time sink, disappearing under the dark blue water as if it had never existed at all. The smooth black stone I kept as a talisman of my idiocy.

"The End" of Harley—*Bad Thing Number One.*

chapter sixteen

*"From the dog's perspective, you're both members of the
same pack, and there can only be one leader. . . . Ambiguity about lead dog status would never occur in the wild;
when it happens at home, your dog learns he can exhibit
beastly behavior and get away with it."*

—SUE OWENS WRIGHT, *150 Activities for Bored Dogs*

AFTER FREDDIE GOT FIXED, WE WATCHED CAREFULLY FOR ANY AND ALL
of those glorious signs that indicated lower testosterone
levels. Less aggression toward dogs, people, even my
kitchen cabinets. But all of the hormone-driven aggressive behaviors that typically subsided in most male dogs post-neutering—
roaming and philandering, attacking male dogs and mounting
females, peeing everywhere to mark their territory—changed not
one whit in Freddie after the procedure. True, Freddie was no
longer capable of spreading his bad seed throughout the canine
population of the Commonwealth of Massachusetts—or anywhere
else—which was undoubtedly a plus. But nothing else about Freddie seemed to have changed at all. If anything, he was worse than
before.

So much for fixing Freddie by, well, fixing him.

The proof that Freddie was as badly behaved as ever came one
Monday evening at my writer's group not long after the New Year.
Just because I'd given up Harley, didn't mean that I was giving up
writing. The Monday Murder Club continued to meet at my house,

and my New Year's resolution was to finish my new novel. A modern retelling of *Little Red Riding Hood* set in a lakeside cottage during a blizzard, it was a story full of storms and woodsmen and wolves. Just like my real life.

Originally, the writer's group was made up of three women and four men. But over time the women had dropped out and now it was just me and the guys. The first to arrive was usually Vaughn, who drove down from New Hampshire in the early afternoon and sat down by the lake with his laptop, working on his thriller until I got home from work. Even in the winter. Vaughn was a native Mainer and a former Marine, so it took more than a little snow and ice and freezing temperatures to rattle him.

When I arrived at the cottage, I let Vaughn in and we tossed down shots of the Maker's Mark whiskey he was always courteous enough to bring with him. Freddie snarled at Vaughn, but one look from the burly Vietnam vet and the cocky beagle backed off.

"That dog is a menace," Vaughn said.

"I know," I said. "I thought getting him fixed would help."

"Hmmph." Vaughn crumpled the brown bag that had held the whiskey into a tight ball and headed for the trashcan under the desk by the stove. When he leaned down to take off the lid, Freddie came out of nowhere, and lunged for Vaughn, fangs bared.

Freddie may have been fast, but Vaughn was faster. With a hard swipe of his right arm, Vaughn sent Freddie sailing across the room. The little dog sprawled on the floor, dazed and confused. He lingered there for a long moment, then struggled to his feet. Freddie regarded Vaughn with a wide brown gaze and a tip of his nose, the canine equivalent of puppy awe. And he never bothered Vaughn again.

But not everyone in my writer's group was that lucky. Steve arrived next, the ubiquitous Dunkin' Donuts to-go cup in one hand and the computer case in the other. Steve was an IT guy by day and a short-story writer by night who churned out more stories in a year than the rest of us wrote in a lifetime.

Freddie and Shakespeare bounded for the front door, barking and growling, and I pulled them away.

"You remember Steve," I told the excited, pushy dogs. "You see him every week, guys." I pulled Freddie away by his lead and pointed to his little round cushion on the floor in front of the armoire in the living room. "Bed," I said firmly.

Shakespeare curled up on his bed as instructed, and watched pridefully as I pushed Freddie's fanny down on his bed.

Steve took his usual place in the rocking chair by the fireplace. Vaughn sat on the church pew on the other side of the room, and I went to the front door to let in Jim and Andy, who'd arrived at the same time and were waiting outside on the front deck.

The dogs abandoned their beds and raced through the kitchen. They beat me to the door, in full attack mode.

"Hold on a minute, guys," I told Jim and Andy through the door. "Mikey!" I dragged the dogs back through the house to Mikey's bedroom, where the increasingly antisocial adolescent was spending more and more of his time. "It's writer's group night, and your dog is going crazy. Take him, please."

Mikey cracked open his door. "Come on, Mom. You know he wants to be out there with you."

"Take him," I said in my no-nonsense voice. "Take them both."

Mikey opened the door wider, and I pushed in the dogs, slamming it shut behind me. I went back to the kitchen and let Andy and Jim into the house. Andy was a tall, gentle man, the only lawyer I'd ever met without a killer instinct. Jim was an ironic English professor with a natural authority that served him well in the classroom. Both wrote erudite mysteries with erudite, crime-solving sleuths as their protagonists.

Jim and Andy joined me on the sectional and the reading began. Each of us took a turn reading twenty pages of our work in progress aloud. Steve went first. But as he regaled us with the latest scene on the Eastern Front in his German World War II novel, Freddie began to whine and wail and scratch and squirm on the other side of Mikey's bedroom door.

"Mom!" Mikey yelled. "Mom! I can't take it anymore." And with that he released the dogs into the living room.

"Bed!" I said and dragged Freddie to his cushion. I pushed his fanny down, and he settled in next to Shakespeare who was already curled up on his cushion, as instructed.

"Go on," I told Steve, and his reading continued uninterrupted until coffee break time. I put on the pot and cut up the apple pie Andy had brought for dessert. The guys took turns using the bathroom. The dogs hovered around me, hoping for a random bite of crust. I always stayed in the kitchen close to the bathroom during the break, as Freddie was more apt than not to forget about the guy in the bathroom, and charge him as if he'd just shown up at the front door.

By the time I passed around the plates of pie, everyone was back in the living room except Andy, last in line to use the facilities. The dogs were back on their beds, drawn into submission with the hope of landing a piece of pie. We were nearly ready to return to the killing fields of Mother Russia when Andy appeared as quietly as a Ninja at the entrance to the living room. Freddie hurtled across the six feet between them and crunched into Andy's knees, shredding his jeans.

"No!" I jumped up, grabbed Freddie's leash, and wrenched the beastly beagle off his feet. He plummeted onto the hardwood, squeaking and squealing. I handed the lead to Vaughn, who quieted Freddie with just one quick jerk of his wrist.

"Andy! Are you all right?" I sank to my knees to check out the damage.

"I'm fine. I guess I just startled him," said Andy, always the gentleman.

"What happened?" Mikey materialized unheralded. "Is Freddie okay?" He looked at Vaughn, who held his disgraceful dog in a death grip.

"He attacked Andy," I told Mikey. "Get him out of my sight, before I kill him."

Vaughn handed Mikey the leash and Mikey picked Freddie up and carried him into his room.

"Do not coddle that beast," I yelled after Mikey. "He's in trouble."

"It's okay," Andy said.

"It's not okay." I was close to tears now. "Mikey loves him but I can't have a dog that bites people. I don't know what to do with him."

"Hmmph!" said Vaughn. "I know what to do with him. Drive him up to Maine, let him loose in the woods, and then take off without him."

"She really doesn't know what to do with him," Steve said to the guys as if I weren't there.

"If he keeps on assaulting people, she's going to have to get rid of him," said Jim.

"She'll never get rid of him," Vaughn said. "She has a negative attachment to that dog."

"Uh, guys, I'm right here." I turned to Vaughn. "I do not have a negative attachment to that dog."

"Okay." Vaughn chuckled. "Whatever you say."

Later that night, after the guys were gone, Mikey emerged from his room with the demon dog from hell.

"Get that dog away from me," I said.

"Please don't get rid of him, Mom." Mikey slipped into the rocking chair, Freddie cradled in his arms.

I threw up my hands. "We have to do something, Mikey. Someone is going to get hurt. I cannot be a party to that. I will not be a party to that."

"I'll train him, Mom, I promise."

"Right." I shook my head. "You don't feed him, you don't walk him, you don't spend hardly any time at all with him anymore. You're certainly not going to train him. Give me a break."

"But, Mom—"

"Andy is a *lawyer.* Your dog attacked a *lawyer* today." I sighed.

"Luckily for us, he's the nicest lawyer in the world, and probably won't sue us. But next time, we might not be so lucky. We are liable for any damage this dog may cause. We could lose the house."

Mikey buried his head in Freddie's soft fur and started to cry.

"Crying won't change anything," I said, more harshly than I intended. "You are increasingly uncooperative lately. You don't do your homework, you don't do your chores, you don't take care of your dog."

"I'm sorry, Mom." Mikey's face was streaked with tears. "I'll do better. I promise."

The sight of my tough-guy teenager in tears moved me more than I could say—or would ever let him know.

"We'll see," I said.

The first thing I did the morning after *Bad Thing Number Two*—Freddie eating Andy's jeans while Andy was still in them—was to call the vet for advice.

"I thought that getting Freddie fixed would help," I told Dr. B, the world's most compassionate and handsomest veterinarian. "But Freddie is more trouble than ever. He actually seems to be getting *worse*."

"I'm sure it is helping," said Dr. B. "But Freddie is at a difficult age—the equivalency of adolescence in dogs."

Great. Now I had two teenaged males to deal with—Freddie and Mikey. Both were testosterone-charged loose cannons who snapped at everything and everyone in sight. I sighed. "What can I do?"

"Let's try a consult with our animal behaviorist."

"What's a . . . ." I paused. I didn't want to sound stupid in front of the world's handsomest vet. "What exactly is an animal behaviorist?"

"Animal behaviorists are experts in the psychology of animal behavior."

A psychologist for dogs. "Are you suggesting that I take Freddie to a doggie shrink?" I laughed.

"Dr. Annie is a veterinarian as well as a fully certified animal behaviorist," Dr. B said, his voice solemn. "She can help us determine what is motivating Freddie's bad behaviors."

Mikey was already seeing a counselor. Now Freddie would be seeing a canine counselor. I laughed harder. Worse, I snorted. Snorted in front of the world's handsomest vet.

"I'm sorry, Dr. B," I said, fighting for control. "I'm sure you're quite right."

chapter seventeen

"The animal behaviorist can prescribe medication for dogs with problems that are too intense or severe to change with training alone."

—GERILYN J. BIELAKIEWICZ, cofounder of Canine University

MY LIFE WAS SO CRAZY EVEN MY *DOG* NEEDED A SHRINK. WHAT WOULD Dr. Annie, celebrated animal behaviorist, think of me? Of Freddie? I wanted us to make a good first impression. So I did everything possible to calm Freddie down before the visit. I ran him through the cranberry bogs with Shakespeare for nearly five miles. I fed him his favorite meal, Purina Dog Chow mixed with olive oil for his coat and topped with a little cheese for extra flavor.

Freddie should have been tired and happy and ready for a nap. But he was agitated, whining incessantly as I put on the leash in preparation for our little outing. Shakespeare was unhappy, too, and unbelieving that Punk Dog was going out while he, Perfect Dog, was forced to remain behind.

I had to drag Freddie out to the car, where he sat solid as a fireplug on the driveway at my feet. He would not get into the car. I begged, cajoled, pleaded. I pulled on the leash and pushed at his unyielding backside.

"Freddie," I finally yelled. "Goddammit, Freddie."

We were running late. I grabbed the little Napoleon around his thick middle and heaved him onto the back seat, whipping the door shut behind him before he could bolt. I raced around the car to the driver's side, slipped in, started the engine, and took off across town, Freddie howling all the way. Every stoplight was a rough scramble as Freddie rushed forward in a bold if misguided effort to maneuver his way into my lap. By the time we reached the vet's office some twenty harrowing minutes later, I was exhausted and pissed. Freddie was just pissed.

He bounded out of the car, free at last and overcome with excitement at the cornucopia of doggie smells that marked this hallowed ground. He lunged for the shrubs that flanked the entry, and I stumbled along behind him. I humored him, allowing him to pee on every bush, buying time before I had to step inside the building with the Dog Who *So* Needed a Shrink.

The waiting area was blessedly empty. I nearly cried with relief, and approached the blond receptionist with a confident smile. The receptionist was a woman; Freddie liked women. There were no men or other dogs to set Freddie off.

"Dr. Annie will be right with you," she said. "Just have a seat."

I led Freddie over to the banquet-style seating that rimmed the room. I sat down, and Freddie sat down. So far so good. I picked up a copy of *Dog Fancy* magazine and flipped through the pages, just your average dog owner with your average dog. I relaxed, and began to read *The Secret Life of Chewers*, an article apparently written with Freddie in mind. I was just coming to the good part when a man wearing an Irish fisherman's cap walked in, his basset hound at his heels.

We had a basset hound when I was a kid. A long-eared, sad-eyed, mellow beauty named Otto who never got worked up over anything—except maybe dinner. This basset rivaled Otto in sanity and serenity. The anti-Freddie.

At the sight of his antithesis, Freddie went crazy. Barking and lunging and jumping. I held on to him tightly, hissing, "Sit, Freddie, sit," over and over again.

The man with the basset sat down across from me and Freddie. The basset paid the badly mannered Freddie no mind at all.

"He's here to see the animal behaviorist," I said, by way of explanation to the man with Buddha Basset.

He looked at me with sympathy. "We had a beagle once. He drove my wife crazy. She walked him for hours every day, but it was never enough. We finally had to get rid of him. She just couldn't take it anymore."

"Right." After the incident with Andy, everyone had told me to get rid of Freddie. My friends, my colleagues, even the Colonel, who loved dogs and was far more likely to blame the owner for any bad dog behavior rather than the dog.

"You tried training him, and that didn't work," Dad said over the phone from Las Vegas. "You tried fixing him, and that didn't work, either. Some dogs just aren't meant to live in polite society. Freddie may be one of them."

The only person left pulling for Freddie was Mikey.

"I love Freddie, Mom," Mikey told me again this morning. "He's a great dog. I'll spend more time training him, I promise. Please give him another chance."

Always a sucker for my youngest child, I relented—and resigned myself to spending thousands of dollars for Freddie therapy.

The man with the basset removed his cap, revealing a finely formed shaved head. With his shiny pate and sensuous mouth, he reminded me of Harley. He caught me staring at him, and I looked away, tears gathering at the back of my eyes. I cursed all bald men with kissable lips and buried my head in Freddie's silky ears. This had the surprising effect of settling us both down.

An interior door opened, and a veterinary assistant with a nametag that read Mary walked out, holding a clipboard. She smiled at me and my dog.

"Freddie?"

At the marvelous sound of his own moniker, Freddie leapt to his feet, and I followed suit. Together we trotted off to meet the inestimable Dr. Annie.

"Wait right here." Mary patted Freddie's head, and then sashayed out of the room, closing the door behind her. Freddie bounced off the walls, sniffing and yelping and groaning with delight. Oh, to be where so many dogs had been before!

I prayed he wouldn't pee on anything.

Dr. Annie came in, a tall, slender woman in her late thirties with long, dark hair that fell over her white vet's coat in shiny waves. *Supermodel meets Dr. Phil.* She introduced herself, and we shook hands.

"So," she said, "this must be Freddie." She leaned down and removed his leash. Then she scratched his ears. He wagged his tail so hard I thought it would fall off. Smart of the little bugger to suck up to the shrink. Maybe he wasn't so loopy, after all.

"He likes you," I said, rather lamely. "He likes women."

She looked at me. "But not men?"

"No. He doesn't like men at all." I sighed. "Of course, he loves my son, he's his dog, really, and he likes my son's friends. He's fine with my dad, and my older son Greg. But that's really it. Any other man he'll attack."

She raised her perfectly plucked eyebrows. "Attack?"

I could understand her skepticism, given the way Freddie was fawning all over her. He certainly didn't look like an attack dog at the moment; with Dr. Annie petting him, he was as docile as Buddha Basset.

So I told her about my writer's group. "They come every Monday. Freddie knows these guys—four of the sweetest guys in the world. But every Monday it's like he's never seen them before in his life. He goes crazy every time." I sighed. "I really don't understand it at all.

We go through the same routine every week. The guys come to the door, I hold Freddie back, and they introduce themselves to him all over again. Freddie calms down . . . but then if they get up and go to the bathroom, Freddie forgets they're there and when they come back into the room, he lunges at them again." I told her about how Freddie attacked Andy, who loved dogs and had gone out of his way to befriend the bullish beagle. "Now Andy brings Freddie dog treats every week. He's determined to win him over. That said, I can't have a dog that goes around biting people—especially lawyers!"

Dr. Annie smiled at me in the same way Mikey's therapist always smiled at me. That is, as if I were some sort of idiot savant. "Of course not." She paused, and stopped petting Freddie. He looked up at her with dismay, tail thumping away, begging for more attention. "Let's put Freddie up on the table."

I lifted thirty-five pounds of squirming beagle up onto the table. Dr. Annie examined Freddie's body leg by leg and organ by organ. The upstart mutt practically wriggled himself wet with pleasure. "And it's just men, mostly, that trigger him?"

No, it's mostly men that trigger me. I was still thinking about Harley, triggered by the man with the basset.

"It's not just men," I said aloud, "it's all sorts of things. People at the door, neighbors, other dogs."

"Does it only happen at home, or in other places as well?"

It happens everywhere. Everywhere there are men who remind me of Harley.

I thought about that. "Freddie barks at everybody—people and dogs—on our walks. But he's mostly fine with Shakespeare, our other dog. And he's fine at the kennel, where we board him when we're out of town. He enjoys the doggie day care. He loves the people and the other dogs there—and they love him."

I'm fine at work, nobody there reminds me of Harley, maybe because there are so few straight men in publishing.

"Well, he *is* a cute little guy." Her examination complete, she pointed to the floor, and I pulled the cute little sycophant down off the table. Freddie sat at her feet, unmoving, in silent adoration.

"Are you single?" asked Dr. Annie.

What sort of question was that? Why was everyone always judging me? Who did Dr. Annie Supermodel Doggie Shrink think she was, anyway?

"Uh, yes, I am." I tried to keep my eyes off the platinum wedding band she wore on the fourth finger of her left hand and the outrage out of my voice, but I'm not sure I altogether succeeded.

"I thought so."

Did this woman have a death wish or what?

"Excuse me?" I managed to mumble.

"We see this phenomenon with single female dog owners a lot. Especially single moms."

Oh, here it comes. Another slam on single moms. Can we never get anything right?

I cast her a defensive glance. "I'm not sure I follow."

Dr. Annie leaned toward me conspiratorially. "I had the same problem with my Doberman when I was a single mom."

When was this veterinary goddess ever a single mom?

"In the absence of a male human, male dogs often try to become the man of the house. They can get very aggressive." Dr. Annie grinned. "After my ex moved out, my dog Baron took his new role as alpha male very seriously. He grew more and more aggressive, especially with the men I dated. Eventually I found someone new—and I had to keep Baron in another room whenever he came over. Once we got married and he moved in, it took Baron awhile to give up his place as alpha male to my husband, but eventually he did."

Ah, the dog shrink may be on to something.

"My adult son Greg lived with us for nearly two years. He worked at home, so he was with the dogs most of the day. Freddie loved him."

I paused, thinking. "It's really since he moved out that Freddie's been so crazy. Do you think that's it?"

"That's probably part of it."

Out in the waiting room a dog began to bark, and Freddie came back to life. He ran to the anteroom door, barking wildly.

I sighed. "I can't get married again just to calm Freddie down."

I can't get married again for any reason. Harley was proof enough of that. My ex-husbands had at least waited until they married me to start lying to me. Harley started on the day we met.

Dr. Annie smiled. "Of course not." She walked over to Freddie. "Come on over here." He stopped barking as if on cue, looked up at her with those big brown eyes, and wagged his tail. "Freddie suffers from separation anxiety and fear-based aggression."

You've got to be kidding me.

Before I could formulate an appropriate response to that, Dr. Annie went on. "Your older son's leaving probably contributed to the separation anxiety, since Freddie loved him and misses him. His leaving also left the man of the house role open—and Freddie's fear-based aggression is a function of his trying to fill that slot."

"Will he grow out of the separation anxiety, like toddlers do?" I had never heard that term applied to anything but toddlers before. Certainly never to a *dog*.

"He'll get used to Greg's absence eventually. Beagles are pack animals, you know." Dr. Annie rubbed Freddie's head. He closed his eyes and curled up his lips in a doggie grin.

"Whenever a member of the pack leaves," continued Dr. Annie, "there's a mourning process—and a reshuffling of the pecking order. It's a good thing that Freddie has Shakespeare to keep him company while you're at work and your younger son is at school. That should help."

Who did I have to keep me company with Harley gone? Mikey was distancing himself from me more every day, as teenagers

*are compelled to do. Was Shakespeare my only consolation as
well? Jesus, I was as bad as Freddie.*

"Okay." I swallowed hard. "What about the fear-based aggression?
Is there anything I can do about that?"

Dr. Annie smiled. "In the absence of an adult male in the household, you need to introduce as many men as you can to Freddie. Have
male friends drop by often. The more men he meets on his home turf,
the better."

"But—" I stopped short. *But I don't want any men on my home
turf, is what I'd almost said. Out loud. To an animal behaviorist.*

"You know," Dr. Annie said gently, "Freddie is affected by your
attitude as well."

Now she's the psychic dog shrink.

"I like men just fine," I said, more than a bit defensively. Freddie
opened his eyes, as if to challenge that statement.

"I'm sure you do." Dr. Annie gave Freddie a final pat, then pulled
out a prescription pad and scribbled away. Freddie watched her as
if his life depended on it. Perhaps it did. "I'm going to recommend
starting Freddie on a low dose of clomipramine. It's an antianxiety
medication that should help ease both his separation anxiety and
fear-based aggression."

You've really got to be kidding.

"You want to give him Puppy Prozac?" I stifled a laugh, which Dr.
Annie mistook as concern.

"It's really quite safe," Dr. Annie assured me. "And while it's not a
panacea, it should help."

*I bet it would. Prozac was a beautiful thing; at least half of the
people I knew were on it. Most couldn't get out of bed without it.
I'd always prided myself on being one of the few writers I knew
who didn't rely on it. But if I kept crying every time I saw a bald
guy . . . .*

Dr. Annie snapped the leash back on Freddie and handed it to
me. Freddie began to whine, sensing the imminent departure of the

beloved object of his affection. "When you stop at the front desk on your way out, Mary will have Freddie's medication ready for you."

"We'll give it a try," I told Dr. Annie. "And if it doesn't work on Freddie, I'll come back and you can write a prescription for me instead."

Dr. Annie did not laugh.

But I did, all the way home, while a newly sedated Freddie snored away on the back seat. I'd given him a dose in the parking lot.

chapter eighteen

"You cannot stop a beagle from howling. You can only redirect him."

—CESAR MILLAN, *Dog Whisperer with Cesar Millan*

T HE NEXT YEAR PASSED IN A BLUR OF INTENSE ACTIVITY AND ANXIETY. I turned fifty, and suffered the usual who-am-I-going-to-marry-when-I-grow-up midlife crisis. My boss quit, an investment firm took over the company I worked for, and I wondered how long I'd have a job myself. Mikey turned sixteen, and discovered sex, drugs, and rap—not necessarily in that order. My daughter Alexis married a lovely French-speaking Swiss Italian man from Sion, Switzerland, named Emmanuel. My son Greg married a Portuguese-speaking Los Angeles Brazilian girl from Natal, Brazil, named Eliane. My mother was diagnosed with colon cancer, and underwent surgery and chemotherapy. *Bad Thing Number Three.*

They didn't tell me about her diagnosis right away. They waited until they could tell me in person. I'd come to Las Vegas for a Ladies Night Out over Easter weekend with Carol and Renee, my two best friends from high school, in honor of my recent fiftieth birthday. My parents adored them both, and often hosted these get-togethers for us in Las Vegas. They all met me at the Las Vegas

Airport with signs proclaiming my advanced age in excessively large type. Carol, always our ringleader, commandeered a wheelchair for me. Renee played "Happy Birthday" on her kazoo. Passersby stopped to stare, as if they hadn't seen anything stranger while visiting the City of Sin. My mother snapped photos as a crowd applauded. I nearly died, first of embarrassment, then of laughter.

That was just the beginning. Carol and Renee planned the perfect weekend for me, celebrating my official entry into midlife with a trip to *Thunder Down Under*, the sizzling "internationally acclaimed male review" at the Excalibur, followed by *Menopause the Musical* at the Luxor.

"We're still hot!" said Carol.

"In more ways than one," added Renee.

My parents, meanwhile, said nothing about my mother's illness, acting as if nothing were wrong. Mom had us dyeing Easter eggs at the kitchen table; Dad regaled us with his animal theories of dating and mating from the recliner parked in the den that adjoined the kitchen.

"Fishing for men," Carol said. "I like it." Carol, who even all these years later still resembled a Creole Cher, had never had to worry about men. They were still falling at her feet, as they'd done since she was sixteen. She married late, but happily.

"No more bottom feeders," said Renee. Renee was the most pragmatic of us three. She married well, and had built a very successful life with Rob, her husband, in the more than twenty years they'd been together.

"Exactly," said the Colonel. "What Paula needs is a trout."

"David was a trout," said Carol, referring to my handsome high-school sweetheart, who was valedictorian of his class at the local Catholic boys' school.

"He's a pediatrician now," I said. "He married the girl he dated after me."

"She broke up with him," called my mother from the stove, where she was making fudge.

"Dale was a trout," said Renee, referring to the Santa Cruz surfer I'd dated between marriages.

"Cute, too," said Carol. "What ever happened to him?"

"I have no idea," I said.

"She broke up with him, too," called my mother again.

Carol and Renee had met nearly every man I'd ever dated since I was fifteen. They had come all the way to Massachusetts when we were living in Salem on the North Shore to meet Thurber. Naturally, he didn't show up.

"Thurber was a carp," Carol said. "I told her to give him up for Lent."

"She didn't," said my mother, spooning a hot lava flow of chocolate into a glass casserole dish.

"Harley was worse." Carol and Renee had liked Harley—and couldn't believe it when they found out that he'd been lying the whole time.

"What's worse than carp?" asked Carol.

"Shark," answered Renee. "Harley was a shark."

"Okay, guys, enough of my miserable love life." I pointed to the dozen eggs left to decorate. "We have work to do."

"But we're not finished," Carol said. "Those were just the boyfriends. We haven't even gotten to the husbands yet."

"Very funny." I sighed. "Okay, okay. If you insist. Dad, tell them about the Golden Retriever."

"Golden Retriever?" Renee looked confused.

"Fishing for the right man is just the beginning," I said. "Training him is where the Colonel's Dog Theory comes in."

"True," Dad said. "You don't want an untrainable husband."

"According to Dad, the most trainable men are the Golden Retrievers."

"My Rob is a Golden Retriever," Renee said. "He makes me breakfast every morning."

"The world's best husband," I agreed.

"I don't get breakfast," Carol said. "But Tim brings me coffee in bed every morning."

"Sounds Golden to me," Dad said.

They all looked at me expectantly.

"All my husbands ever brought me was trouble."

"Dobermans," the Colonel said. "Always with the Dobermans."

"Joel is not a Doberman," my mother said.

"We never met Joel," Carol said.

"The original Golden Retriever," Dad said.

"She broke up with him," my mother said. "For you know who."

"You left a Golden for a Doberman." Renee laughed. 'What were you thinking?" Everyone laughed now.

"Hilarious."

"I'm sure you'll meet another Golden Retriever soon," said Renee. "I'll light a candle for you."

"Me, too," said Carol.

I laughed. "Mom's lit a million candles for me. Right, Mom?"

Mom appeared at the kitchen table, the glass pan of luscious fudge in her mittened hands. "Yes. But we need all the prayers we can get." She looked up toward heaven. "I don't want to die knowing she's still alone."

The sudden seriousness of her tone brought us all up short.

"Mom—"

"We have something to tell you," Mom said.

That something was colon cancer. They'd caught it early and the prognosis was good. Surgery and six months of chemotherapy in pill form should do the trick.

"I won't even lose my hair," said my mother.

"Oh, Mom," I said, choking back tears. "I'm so sorry. Are you in any pain?"

"I'm fine," she said. "Everything will be all right. Don't worry."

"I'm worried," I said. "Of course I am going to worry." I paused. "I can't believe you didn't tell me right away. You need to tell me these things right away."

"We wanted to tell you in person," my mother said. "We knew you were coming out here in just a couple of weeks. And we knew that Carol and Renee would be here. We thought it would be easier for you that way."

"Mom, it's not about me," I said. "It's about doing what makes it easier for *you*. What can I do for *you*?"

"Not much, really," Mom said. "You need to go home and take care of Mikey. Daddy and the doctors will take care of me."

Before I left for home, I took my father aside.

"Dad, you need to keep me informed every step of the way. One phone call, and I'm on the next plane. . . ."

The Colonel looked as grim as I had ever seen him. "Don't worry, I will call you. I'm not going through this with your mother alone." His voice cracked, and I hugged him for a long, long time.

chapter nineteen

"There are going to be lots of things in your dog's life that he wants (or wants to chase), but isn't allowed, either for his own safety or for the safety of the objects in question."

—JENNIFER BRIDWELL, *The Everything Dog Obedience Book*

FOR NOW, FREDDIE WAS THE LEAST OF MY PROBLEMS. WHICH IS NOT to say that he was much better behaved when medicated than when he was clean and sober. True, the Puppy Prozac did calm the naturally hyper dog down enough to cure him of eating shoes and peeing on furniture. But he remained as territorial as ever, aggressive toward other dogs and most all male humans, friend and foe alike.

I just didn't have the time or the inclination to do much about it. I was so busy working and worrying that I even let Freddie's prescription run out—and never bothered refilling it. If there were any difference in his behavior off the drug, I didn't notice it.

In truth, I probably wasn't noticing much of anything that went on at home. Work was my escape from cancer, teenagers, and bad dogs. I took on more hours, more authors, more projects. I traveled more often on business as well: New York, Los Angeles, San Diego, London, Cannes.

When I wasn't working, I was working out. Every night I came home from the office, slipped on some workout clothes, and took Shakespeare and the newly medicated Freddie for a long walk through the bogs. I hired a boxing trainer, bought an eighty-pound heavy bag, and hung it on the back porch. All summer long while Mikey was out in California with his father, I banged that bag long into the night. If Freddie were howling, I didn't even hear him.

I did not date. I knew now that life was too short for bad relationships—and until I could figure out how to have a good relationship, there was no point in having one at all.

So I gave up men, at least temporarily. I was playing it safe, as I'd had enough surprises this year. I couldn't bear another shock.

Yet, no matter how you try to safeguard yourself against life's little aftershocks, the earth still moves under your feet when you least expect it. Mikey came home with the startling news that his father and Miss Priss were breaking up. His father had moved out and was living in his shop. Naturally I was delighted that it didn't work out. It took seven years, but blessed with a killer instinct I did not possess, my Doppelganger eventually brought my ex to his knees.

"Karma!" I told anyone who would listen, "Karma in my lifetime!"

My ex had done so much against me that I felt obliged to hate him for all eternity. My father had once told me that my inability to hate the people who had wronged me was a character flaw. But after that terrible custody battle, I had no trouble hating my ex. In fact, my loathing of the man was a point of pride on my part. Ever since Mikey and I had made our final escape to New England, whenever anyone told me I should be charitable toward my ex, I would reply: "Sorry, I'm old-fashioned. I believe in hating my ex-husbands."

Thanks to Miss Priss, it was a rule I followed religiously—and easily. But now she was gone—and I was happy for Mikey and for my ex. I wanted Mikey to have a good relationship with his father; I knew from Greg and his dad how much a young man could suffer without it. I didn't want that to happen to Mikey. With Miss Priss out of the picture, I figured it would be easier for Mikey and his father to have that good relationship.

But that would have to wait until vacation. Now Mikey was back home with me. School started and life got back to normal for us both. Sort of. The economy was slowing down and my well water pump was dying and without Miss Priss's money my ex was running more late than usual on child support. I was going broke like everyone else in America.

Mikey wanted an iPhone for Christmas, and I didn't want to disappoint him. This extravagantly expensive electronic toy would put me back $400—$400 I didn't exactly have. But I was determined to give it to him, as I was always determined to give the kid what he wanted, when I could.

But I couldn't quite pull this iPhone present off on my own. So I swallowed my pride and decided to contact my ex to see if we could get it for our son together. He owed me money, Miss Priss was out of my son's life for good, and my mother was alive and well and cancer-free, so despite the world's growing economic woes I was feeling charitable. The character flaw my father had identified was reasserting itself. I was unable to hate my ex any more.

It had been years since my ex and I had had a regular conversation. Our communication had been limited to e-mails detailing Mikey's flight information and/or delinquent child support payments. When Mikey was in California, I contacted him directly on his cell phone when I wanted to talk to him. There was rarely a reason for me to talk to my ex.

My calling him now would represent a shift so significant that it scared me. I didn't want to hate my ex, I didn't want to hate anyone, but hating him was so much safer than not hating him. It's not that I was worried about becoming one of those, "Oh, we're divorced, but let's be pals and all celebrate major holidays together, la di da" kind of fools. I couldn't imagine doing that.

But I could imagine opening the Pandora's box of remorse and ruin I'd locked up and buried deep in my heart the day my lawyer told me never to come back to California again. My ex and I had always suffered a passionate association, for better or worse . . . until that protracted, financially and emotionally devastating legal battle blew us apart.

But Mikey was going to get that iPhone.

So I called his father, and the man who usually answered, "Oh, if it isn't the bitter divorcée," instead said, "Hi."

A modest start, to be sure, but that little "Hi" led to "How are you," which led to—shocker of all shockers—"I'm sorry."

I'm sorry? My ex was apologizing? To me? I was stunned. More impressive, I was speechless.

Since I couldn't speak, he did. He talked a long time, and I listened—each an unprecedented act, respectively. He told me how much he'd missed me and Mikey when I'd divorced him and moved to Boston, how angry and hurt he was when I'd taken his son away, how he'd schemed with Miss Priss to get his son back no matter what the price. The price had been high.

"I'm sorry, too," I whispered.

"What?"

"You heard me," I said, and hung up.

I never thought I'd ever apologize to that man for anything. I blamed him for ruining our marriage. I blamed him for ruining our family. I blamed him for ruining my life. I blamed him for everything—but anyone who's ever been married knows that there's always a lot of blame to go around.

I called him back, as I'd forgotten to ask him about the iPhone for our son. He agreed that we should buy it for Mikey together and that collaboration prompted another, stranger joint venture. We spent hours on the phone, talking and texting and e-mailing. We examined every aspect of our relationship, past and present, good and bad, fated and doomed. In the end, we agreed to a truce.

We even went to lunch together in Las Vegas, the three of us, the day after Christmas. Mikey and I had come to stay at my folks' house, where our family was gathering for the holidays. Usually Mikey would fly to California on Christmas morning, but this year his dad offered to drive to Vegas to pick him up, so we could give him the iPhone together.

"This is weird," Mikey said as we walked into the BBQ restaurant at a casino near my folks'.

"Very weird," I agreed. The last time my ex and I had been in the same room together was in court six years before.

I'd dressed very carefully for this lunch, donning a classic little black dress that I'd had since we were married—and that I knew he'd always liked. Alexis had fixed my hair, and the high-heeled pumps I wore were brand-spanking new.

He looked exactly the same: tall, lean, handsome in a sort of craggy Sam Elliott kind of way. Older, balder, wearier—but still the man I had once loved beyond all reason.

I waited for that twist in my gut, the one I couldn't resist even when I knew better. The one that I'd always felt with my ex. And admittedly still did, although now I believed it was the pull of anxiety, not attraction.

He grinned at me, and gave Mikey a big hug.

"Hi, Dad." Mikey stepped back. "Uh, here's Mom."

"You look great," my ex said, and gave me a hug, too.

That was one of the things I'd always liked best about my ex. He always thought I looked great, and told me so, even when it wasn't true. But it was true enough today.

In the restaurant, we ordered ribs and pulled-pork sandwiches and talked about Mikey's iPhone. We gave our son the contract we'd put together, the one that specified that he do his homework and all his chores to earn unlimited text messaging every month.

"Whatever," Mikey said, and we, the proud parents, beamed at one another.

Mikey excused himself, ostensibly to use the bathroom, but more likely to text every girl in the eleventh grade unobserved.

"You look great," my ex said again.

"So do you," I said.

He ran a well-shaped hand through his thinning dark hair. I'd always loved his hands. "Except for that male-pattern baldness."

I laughed. "All men should go bald. It's the only consolation for us old broads."

"You're no old broad. You're beautiful. You've always been beautiful."

I could feel myself blushing. Blushing!

He leaned across the table and lowered his voice. "You were my own personal Marilyn Monroe."

And you were my own personal Heathcliff, I thought. But I didn't say it out loud. I nearly kissed him on the spot. But fortunately Mikey chose that moment to reappear. We had chocolate cake for dessert. My ex picked up the check, and drove me back to my folks' house.

"Have fun with your Dad, sweetheart," I said to Mikey as I got out of the truck.

His father got out, too, and gave me one last hug.

"Bye, boys," I said, just as I had done when Mikey was little and we were still married.

"Bye, babe," my ex said.

Later, when we were back home in Massachusetts, Mikey told me that lunch was the only civilized meal he ever remembered the three of us sharing together. We made a new, happier memory for us all that day, a sweet counterpoint to the many unhappy memories that had come before.

No, we didn't live happily ever after. At least not as the couple and family we'd once been. But Mikey got his iPhone, and we got closure.

My ex and Mikey went back to California to celebrate New Year's together.

And I went back to New England to get a life.

chapter twenty

"What the dog clearly knows is to anticipate punishment when the owner appears wearing a look of displeasure. What the dog does not know is that he is guilty.

He just knows to look out for you."

—ALEXANDRA HOROWITZ, *Inside of a Dog*

S T. JUDE MUST HAVE BEEN LISTENING TO MY MOTHER'S PRAYERS. OR maybe it was the lighting of all those candles. By the time spring rolled around, a good-looking single guy around my age moved in right down the street.

In our neighborhood as in all neighborhoods, there was one neglected house that all the other homeowners on the street complained brought down their property values. On the isolated road that ran along the lake where we lived, that house was a tiny cottage with peeling paint, junk cluttering the driveway, and thigh-high weeds for a yard. Worse, the tenants were often seen being escorted from the property by local law enforcement, only to return a few days later. But to our collective relief, eventually they disappeared for good, and a "for sale" sign went up on the lot. Not that we could imagine anyone actually buying the house in its unkempt condition.

The little cottage stood empty for months. Then one happy day, a truck pulled up, a tall, dark-haired guy with long limbs and a ready smile got out, and the renovation began. He gutted the place and transformed it from derelict cabin to lakeside jewel in a matter of weeks. All of us neighbors were thrilled and predisposed to like the bachelor who'd cleaned up the worst house on the block. Me, especially.

I met him as I walked Shakespeare and Freddie down the road to the bogs for our daily excursion into the great outdoors. If only Freddie would let this be a cute meet, just like in all those romantic comedies I loved. Harry meeting Sally on the carpool ride to New York City. Alvy Singer meeting Annie Hall on a blind tennis date. Shakespeare meeting Viola dressed as an actor auditioning for Romeo.

Shakespeare wagged his tail at our new neighbor. But Freddie, still suspicious of any man outside our immediate family, growled and barked, lunging on the leash. I held the aggressive little dog back while I shouted a welcome over Freddie's loud howls, then moved quickly on my way. I'd have to chat him up later, when Freddie was safely contained in the big doghouse that was once known as my garage.

That evening, to my delight, the good-looking new neighbor knocked on our door, prompting the usual cacophony of growls and barks and howls from Freddie. Even the Puppy Prozac hadn't prompted Freddie to respond better to strangers at the door. Freddie remained a sweet and loving dog to women everywhere and the few men whom he deemed family—and an aggressive and unpredictable hound from hell to most every other man on the planet, neighbors included.

I was thinking about building a fence around my property; with Freddie around, maybe good fences did make good neighbors. Not to mention then I could add a doggie door, giving Freddie twenty-four-hour access to the outdoors, which might cut back on his "accidents." But I worried about ruining the view. I'd have to talk to Joel about it. I held Freddie back as I answered the door.

"Hi," said the neighbor we'll call Jesse.

"Hi," I said, holding on to Freddie for dear life. "Sorry."

"No problem, I like dogs."

"Yeah, well, he doesn't like men much."

Jesse looked at me and grinned. "That's not good."

"No." I laughed. "It's not."

"I'd love to come in and see your place."

"Oh, of course." We'd all seen every inch of his house during the remodel. I guess this turnabout was fair enough play. I backed away from the door with Freddie. "Sure, come on in." I pulled Freddie into the living room, and with Shakespeare on my heels, pointed to their doggie pillows in the corner.

"Bed," I said. Since sleeping was Freddie's favorite pastime—after eating, that is—he curled right up next to Shakespeare, keeping one eye on Jesse as he did.

I turned to Jesse. "Would you like a beer or something?"

"Sure. Thanks." Jesse sat down on my couch in front of the fireplace as if he owned the place. "This is a great house."

"Thanks. You've certainly done a lot with yours." I handed him a beer and sat down at the other end of the L-shaped sectional.

With that opening, Jesse was off and running. He told me how he'd inherited some money, checked out the local foreclosures, and found the house on our street. What a mess the place was, the complete remodeling he had to do, how much hard work it took to make it a habitable home. "But it was all worth it," he said. "I always wanted to live on this lake."

"Yes, it's lovely here."

"So," he said, suddenly switching gears and leaning toward me. "You're single, aren't you?"

"Uh, yes."

"Wow, what luck." He leered at me. "I move into my new place, and right away I meet a babe." And with that lame preamble he fell on me, all tongue and hands and heavy breathing.

He wasn't that cute. I pushed him off me and stood up. "You need to leave now."

He held his hands up. "Hey, just being neighborly, you know?"

"You need to leave now," I repeated.

He started toward me, his arms open now in a welcoming embrace. "I mean, you're single, I'm single—"

"Now," I said, with a firmness that brought Freddie to his feet. The fierce little beagle rocketed across the room, fangs bared.

"Whoa," called Jesse, backing up.

I caught Freddie by the collar as he zipped past me, just as he lunged at Jesse's crotch. I jerked him back just as his jaws began to close around Jesse's hands, which the terrified man had cupped around his private parts.

"You can let yourself out."

"Maybe another time," Jesse said, regaining his composure as he slipped out my front door, Freddie howling and growling all the while, Shakespeare's deep baritone bark now adding to the din.

"I don't think so," I said as I locked the door behind him.

"That's enough," I told the dogs, and Shakespeare stopped barking. Freddie, naturally, did not.

"Enough," I said again. Freddie quieted down, gazed up at me with those big, innocent brown eyes, and then looked down, penitent, ready for his punishment. This is the part where I usually chastised him with more than one "Bad dog! Bad dog! Bad dog!"

I should have been ashamed that Freddie had snapped at yet another man. That was three guys now: Steve, Andy, and Jesse. But actually I was pleased. This time Freddie had bitten someone who deserved it. I wondered if he knew the difference.

"I'm giving you the benefit of the doubt," I told Freddie, as I opened the fridge and pulled out two slices of American cheese, Shakespeare's and Freddie's favorite "people food" treat.

While the dogs chomped down dessert, I poured myself a glass of wine and raised it in a mock toast to the world's worst beagle:

"To Freddie, who knows a good neighbor when he sees one—or not."

Freddie wagged his tail in acknowledgement of my praise—and promptly lifted his leg against the kitchen cabinet.

Time to build that fence, I thought. *If and when I can afford it.*

Which meant maybe next year, unless Joel built it for me. I'd talked to him about a new pergola for the wisteria that had outgrown its small arbor, too. But the recession was in full swing now; between no child support, the new no-raise policy at work, and topped-out credit cards, I was strapped, and working harder than ever just to stay afloat. I was traveling more for work, too, but I didn't complain. This was no time to lose my job.

The economy aside, there was some good news that summer of 2008. My daughter Alexis was pregnant with my first grandchild. She came to visit us at the cottage, five months pregnant and very susceptible to malodorous beagles.

"Oh, Mom, Freddie smells so bad."

"Oh, honey, I'm so sorry." I'd borne three kids; I knew how sensitive to scent a woman could be when she was carrying a child. "I know how you feel. When I was pregnant with you, it was Chinese food. One whiff and I'd toss my wontons."

"Can't you give him a bath or something?"

"Sure. I just gave the dogs baths, but I can give them another one."

"It's just Freddie, Mom, Shakespeare is fine."

"He's a hound. They have a unique gamy odor."

"I'll say." Alexis turned a little green under her beautiful blond paleness.

"Let me get the Febreze," I said, and ran for the kitchen.

Outside, while Alexis sat by the lake, I hosed Freddie down with the stuff. Over the years I'd tried everything to tone down Freddie's raunchy perfume: dog-grooming sprays, Murphy's Oil soap, even softener sheets for the dryer. But nothing really worked, at least not for long.

"Let's hope this does the trick," I told the stinky little dog, who howled piteously as I squirted him with the deodorizing cleanser. "Because if it's you or my grandchild, it won't look very good for you, my little pretty."

Freddie and I went through two bottles of Febreze that visit, but it was worth it.

The next week I was going to Los Angeles for a business trip. I would see Greg and his wife Eliane while I was there, and my folks were driving over from Vegas so we could all be together. Unbeknownst to the family, Alexis planned to fly there with me, as a special surprise for everyone.

There was only one complication: Mikey. Now sixteen, he'd chosen to come home early from his dad's so he could spend some time hanging out with his friends before school started. He didn't want to go to California with me and Alexis; he'd just come home from there. But I had my doubts about leaving him alone.

"I'm a big boy now," he told me in not-so-mock exasperation when I protested the idea of leaving him alone at home with the animals for five days.

"I don't know," I said. Usually I planned most of my business trips while Mikey was away visiting his father. If I did have to travel while he was home, I never stayed away that long, and I arranged for a friend—read babysitter—to stay with him. But this was an important trip I couldn't cut short.

"You let Alexis and Greg stay home alone when they were sixteen."

"Yes, but that was different," I said.

"Because I was perfect," Alexis teased her little brother.

"Everyone knows you're the perfect one." Mikey scowled. "But what about Greg?"

"Not the perfect one," Alexis said.

"Alexis kept him out of trouble," I said.

"Yeah, right." Mikey shook his head.

"Well, I tried," Alexis said. "Who's going to keep you out of trouble?"

"I'm not Greg."

"No, but—"

Mikey cut me off. "I'm a junior now, Mom. Give me a break."

I acquiesced, as I did so often these stressful days, and instead simply asked my friend Susan to drop by and check up on him while I was gone. That, coupled with my frequent check-in phone calls, e-mails, and texts, would be enough supervision. Or so I hoped.

Alexis and I landed in Los Angeles on a stereotypically warm and smoggy day. Greg picked us up, thrilled to see his sister. He dropped me off at the convention center, and then took Alexis back to his apartment to surprise Eliane and her grandparents.

That night we gathered at a Mexican restaurant for dinner. Alexis and my mother, Greg and my father, Eliane and I, all together at a big round table, drinking margaritas and eating guacamole, Alexis sans tequila. I called Mikey, so he could talk to everybody. And to check up on him.

"Everything's fine, Mom." He cleared his throat. "Better than fine. As a matter of fact, there's a surprise for you when you come back."

"A surprise?"

"Yeah."

"What surprise?"

"Can't say."

"But—"

"I promised, Mom." Mikey paused. "Gotta go. Tell everybody goodbye for me."

The surprise was the talk of the dinner that night.

"There's only one thing I can think of," I told my mother. "The pergola."

"What pergola?"

"The pergola Mom needs to replace the arbor that's falling down," Alexis explained.

"Where the wisteria and grape vines have grown wild."

My mother smiled. "You're talking about Joel, aren't you?"

I grinned. "Maybe. It would be just like him to build it for me while I was gone."

"Very romantic," my daughter-in-law said. Eliane was Brazilian, and appreciated such grand gestures.

I took a swig of margarita. "He'll build me a pergola, but he won't marry me."

"No man builds a woman a pergola unless he's in love with her," my mother said.

"That's what you said when he tiled my bathroom floor, Mom." I laughed. "Nothing happened."

"But the floor looks good," Greg said.

"So will the pergola," the Colonel said.

"I could be wrong," I said. "But hope I'm not."

"Joel will come through," my mother said, ever hopeful.

When I came home five days later, a beautiful pergola stood to greet me, draped in wisteria and grape vines.

"It's lovely," I told Joel.

"I'm glad you like it," Joel said.

"You know, in some countries, building a woman a pergola is tantamount to a proposal of marriage."

"Thank God we live in America," Joel said.

Joel wasn't the only one waiting for me when I got home. My neighbor Steve came over as soon as Joel left.

"Mikey had a party while you were gone," he told me. "The police came."

"Oh my God." I didn't understand. "I told him he could only have one friend over at a time while I was gone."

"There were literally hundreds of people here," Steve said. "Cars everywhere."

"Mikey doesn't even *know* hundreds of people."

"The cops said somebody put the party up on Facebook, and

that drew them in from as far away as New Hampshire. And they weren't all kids either. There were college kids and people in their mid-twenties here, too." Steve looked at me. "When the police came, they all scattered. I found a couple of kids hiding under my boat."

"I can't believe it." I shook my head. "Thanks for telling me. I'm going to go kill him now."

"He didn't mean for it to happen," Steve said. "Things got out of control, and he didn't know how to stop it."

"I appreciate that," I told Steve. "But I'm still going to kill him."

I found Mikey inside cleaning the kitchen. But doing the dishes wasn't going to get him out of this one.

"I'm going to change my clothes and then we're going to talk," I told him. I went into my room, and screamed.

Mikey came running, Shakespeare and Freddie on his heels. "What's wrong?"

"Someone has been in my room." I pointed to my bed, which was a mess, clothes and covers amiss. I pointed to the top drawer of my nightstand, which was half open. I pulled it out all the way. It was empty. "My jewelry is gone."

"I'm so sorry, Mom." Mikey seemed shell-shocked.

"My pearls, my engagement rings, my diamond tennis bracelet." I caught my breath. "The gold necklace your father gave me when you were born."

"I'm so sorry, Mom."

"Is that all you can say? What else is gone?"

Mikey dropped his eyes and bowed his head. Presumably in shame.

"Who did you let into our house?"

"I, I—"

"Steve said you had a party. He said hundreds of kids were here."

Mikey shook his head. "I didn't even know most of them, Mom. I never invited them. It was just supposed to be a few friends from school."

"Right. And which of those friends robbed us blind?"

"It wasn't anyone I knew, Mom." He threw up his hands. "They just showed up. I didn't know what to do."

"That's why you're not allowed to have more than one friend over when I am not here," I said harshly.

"I know. I know." Mikey's voice cracked. He was close to tears.

I sighed. "Let's make an inventory of everything that's gone. And then I'm calling the police."

The total tally was nearly $20,000 worth of jewelry, video games, plus the kayak and the canoes, which a couple of the more enterprising thieves had used as getaway vessels when the police showed up. My insurance only covered $3,000 of that. Local law enforcement confirmed Steve's story and asked Mikey to name the older party crashers, the kids most likely to have stolen our stuff.

"Mom, I can't—"

"Tell him, Mikey. And call all your friends and ask them who else was here."

The police officer listened with interest to the people Mikey and his friends named. Apparently one of his friends had a sibling who was a drug addict responsible for a string of break-ins in the area.

"I can't believe it," I told the officer. "Not here."

"Everywhere," he said. "One kid texts another, and the next thing you know, the pros are driving in from miles away to rip you off."

That evening I sat with Mikey and the dogs in the living room, Alice on my lap.

"Where were the dogs when all this was going on?"

"They were here."

"They didn't bark . . . or anything?"

"No."

"Unbelievable!" I looked at Freddie. "You attack my writer's group, but you let criminals come in and steal everything that's not tied down."

"Mom—"

"You and Freddie are both grounded," I said. "Until the end of time."

chapter twenty-one

"First you learn a new language, profanity; and second you learn not to discipline your dogs when you're mad, and that's most of the time when you're training dogs."

—Lou Schultz, renowned trainer of Alaskan Huskies

IT WAS TIME FOR OBEDIENCE TRAINING . . . AGAIN. AND NOT JUST FOR Freddie, but for Mikey, too. I knew what to do with Mikey. I'd been through it with Greg when he was a teenager. I just never thought that I'd have to do it with Mikey. I always thought that I'd have backup. That is, I always thought I'd have a husband.

"He needs a father," I told Joel, who was back at the house expanding the front deck.

"Too late for that," Joel said, and kept on banging nails.

Joel was right. Too late for a dad. Mikey would have to make do with me. I'd be his mother, his father, and the Colonel all rolled into one.

"No iPhone. No Internet access. No video games." I packed up the Xbox 360 and locked up the laptop computer with the wireless connection, which the thieves had apparently considered too big to carry. I removed the few video games and CDs they'd also left behind, and canceled his allowance for the foreseeable future. "And the remote is mine. Prepare to watch a lot of *Masterpiece Theatre*."

"You're not serious." Mikey rolled his eyes.

"You don't leave the house. And you don't have friends over."

"For how long?"

"Forever." I glared at him. "Life as you know it is over."

"But—"

"Do you like your hair, Curly?" Curly was the nickname the girls at school had given Mikey, in honor of his burnished brown locks.

For once, Mikey didn't say anything. He knew that when his brother Greg was his age, I'd shaved his head in a last-ditch effort to discipline the rebellious teenager. Greg loved his hair—and the ploy had worked.

I couldn't threaten to shave the beagle's head. So I took Freddie to see Dr. B instead. I'd read that there were new, improved drugs for badly behaved dogs, drugs far stronger than the meds Dr. Annie had prescribed for him and I'd long ago abandoned for lack of results. Maybe a miracle drug could calm Freddie down enough to be receptive to obedience training.

But once we got to the animal hospital, Freddie seemed intent on proving me wrong. He waltzed into the lobby at my side, as graciously as a show dog on the floor of Westminster. I stopped when I realized there were other people and other dogs in the room. Freddie stopped, too, and we stood there as if in a tableau.

There were two men, one gripping twin leashes bearing twin dachshunds yapping a mile a minute, and the other holding a cat carrier on his knees. The Siamese inside meowed loudly in return. Freddie did not growl or bark or pull on his lead. I sat down and he sat down. I was quiet and he was quiet. When I got up to follow the receptionist into an examination room, Freddie got up, too, and trotted along beside me, canine escort extraordinaire.

When Dr. B came into the room, Freddie greeted him with a friendly brown-eyed gaze and a happy wag of his tail.

I told Dr. B about the killer beagle's run-in with my neighbor Jesse.

"I've got to get this dog under control once and for all," I told Dr. B. "I've heard that you've got better drugs now for aggressive dogs."

"That's true." Dr. B scratched Freddie's growing belly. "But I don't think Freddie needs that sort of assistance anymore. He's greatly improved."

Even I had to admit that he'd been far better this trip than he'd ever been before.

"Our Freddie is finally growing up," Dr. B said. "He's nearly five now, and his adolescence is behind him."

"Then what do you suggest? He may be better but he's not ready for prime-time obedience classes. We tried that before."

"He's not ready for a class with other dogs," agreed Dr. B. "But I think he'll do just fine with private lessons." He handed me a card. "This trainer is very good. Give it a try."

"But—"

"If it doesn't work out, we'll consider a new medication."

"Okay." I smiled, and shook the handsome doctor's hand. "Thank you."

He gave Freddie a final pat. "Good boy, Freddie. Good boy!"

The obedience trainer came to the cottage three days later for Freddie's first lesson. We stood outside in the warm October sun with the dogs. Karen was a cheerful, no-nonsense woman about my age. She wore jeans and a sweatshirt and a carpenter's belt around her hips filled with doggie treats.

Naturally, Freddie loved her.

"So this is our little troublemaker?" she asked, petting the model hound, who stood alert and pert, yet relaxed on the leash.

"Yes."

"Has he learned any commands yet?"

I shrugged. "He'll sit, but only for popcorn."

Karen laughed. "Oh, yes. Beagles are particularly motivated by food."

"Sit," she told Freddie, and he sat. Karen rewarded the little sycophant with a treat.

"He likes you. He likes women."

"But not men?" Karen asked.

At that moment, Joel came out of the garage with a saw.

Joel had finished rebuilding and expanding the deck, and was now building a fence. A fence that would give the canine kings of the septic mound free rein in the side yard. He'd done similar work all around the house—from reshingling the cottage exterior to paving my front walkway. Not to mention the pergola.

But that didn't endear him to Freddie. Freddie lunged forward on the leash, snarling and growling, as if he'd never seen Joel before.

"This is what we need to fix," I told Karen. "Joel is here all the time; there's no reason for Freddie to go after him. He knows Joel."

"I hate that dog," Joel said evenly. Joel was a cat man. He tolerated Shakespeare, but his heart belonged first to Isis and now to Alice, as well as to his own cat, Kirby.

Karen turned her back on Freddie. The little dog stopped barking at Joel, and jumped up on Karen. She moved away, turning her back on him again. He dropped all four paws back to the ground, and stood there, ears and tail up, expectant.

"Sit," Karen said in a firm voice. And Freddie sat. So did Shakespeare. I was tempted to sit myself. I wondered if she'd give me a treat if I did.

Karen gave the dogs each a treat and then turned to me. "Whenever the dog does something you don't want him to, don't react. Simply turn your back on him and wait. Ignore him until he behaves the way he is supposed to behave."

For several minutes, we practiced sitting and rewarding, ignoring and waiting. I found the sitting and rewarding part much easier than the ignoring and waiting part.

"You have to train yourself as much as you train the dog," Karen explained.

I laughed. "And you thought beagles were bad!"

"Freddie's not bad," Karen said. "He's just used to getting his way. You have to show him that you're in charge."

Freddie sat there, happy as a clam, his lip curled in a grin. He loved this sitting and rewarding game.

"Let's work on greeting," Karen said. "Do you think Joel would be willing to help us?"

"Uh, sure." I looked around.

"I heard you," Joel said, putting the saw down and coming over to join us in the road in front of the house. "What can I do?"

"We're going to practice what's called Treat and Retreat," Karen said. "Here's how it works." Karen gave the leash to me. "Hold him loosely on the lead."

I did as I was told. Karen backed up a few feet, then tossed a doggie goodie onto the ground. "Let him come forward to get the treat."

Freddie trotted forward and gobbled up the treat with his usual greedy good humor. He looked up at Karen, who'd moved back a couple of feet while the motivated mutt was chomping down his canine candy. And so this Treat and Retreat shuffle continued.

Karen threw another goodie between them, and again moved back as I allowed Freddie to move forward to eat the treat. The third time she did not toss the goodie on the ground but rather held the treat in her open palm, and he advanced happily to lick it up. She waited for him to finish eating, then rewarded the proud pooch with lots of praise and petting.

"Okay," Karen said. "I think we're ready."

Karen directed Joel to take her place across from me and Freddie. She gave him some treats from her carpenter's belt. "Now, make sure that Freddie sees that you have the treat in your hand before you pitch it."

Joel dropped slowly into a squat. He held up a large hand, the small goodie tucked between his thumb and forefinger, dwarfed by the thick digits.

"Freddie," he said in his usual calm, deep voice.

Freddie looked at him with suspicion, then sniffed. And sniffed again. He eyed the treat with a covetous look. And Joel with only slightly less suspicion.

Joel tossed the treat on the ground. Freddie advanced, and I along with him. He munched down the beefy bonbon while Joel retreated as instructed.

"Repeat," Karen ordered, and we all obeyed.

By the third time, Freddie was regarding Joel with an affection he'd never shown before.

"If you feel comfortable," Karen said to Joel, "try offering him the treat in your open palm. But only if you feel comfortable."

Joel placed a big piece of canine candy on the broad width of his sizable hand. Freddie and I slid forward. I held my breath. Joel smiled at me, a sardonic grin I knew well.

Freddie sniffed Joel's monster paw, and then carefully nudged the candy with his wet nose. Once reassured that it was indeed a treat and not a trick, Freddie joyfully nibbled it up in seconds, licking Joel's palm for good measure.

"Oh my God," I said.

"Good boy," said Joel, and patted the satisfied little hound on the head.

Karen watched with interest. "Now, that was brave of Joel to pet him. You'll want to practice this with other people, like your neighbor Steve. But warn them not to try and pet the dog until they feel ready."

"One lesson and you have Freddie eating out of Joel's hand," I said. "You are a goddess."

"As you can see, Freddie is perfectly trainable with the right approach," Karen said. "You can teach him to sit and stay, high-five, even ring a bell when he wants to go out."

"Really," I said, unbelieving, even in the face of today's miracles.

"Just remember," Karen said. "Practice makes perfect."

If It Ain't Broke, Don't Fix It:

idiomatic expression, leave well enough alone

chapter twenty-two

"Dogs live in the moment. They don't reminisce about the past or worry about the future; therefore, they can move on from unstable behavior very quickly—if we let them."

—CESAR MILLAN, *Be the Pack Leader*

T JOEL'S INSISTENCE, I RENTED A DUMPSTER AND CLEANED OUT MY garage. Or, rather, he cleaned out my garage. I got home just in time to save a (very rusted) wrought iron antique ice cream dinette set and a box of old journals. I read through these old notebooks, and came across a Post-it on which I'd made three wishes seven years before when we were living in Salem on the North Shore of Massachusetts, not long after Mikey and I made our final escape from California.

In bright red ink I'd scrawled the following hopeful list:

1. House
2. Horse
3. Husband

Seven years later, I had the house. And Mikey and I were happy here. I didn't have a horse, but then I'd never had a pony as a child either. I would live. I'd begun dating again, this time with the cautionary voice of my mother intoning "intense" in my head with every romantic move I made. But there was no husband in sight—and for the first time since puberty, that was fine by me.

Mikey was graduating from high school in the spring; as a senior he'd taken a sudden interest in the world beyond Lytton and was planning a future as a mathematician. He was the lead scorer on his high school's MATHletes team, and would leave to study game theory at college after graduation. (Proving that all the time he wasted playing video games throughout his adolescence might actually pay off. Eventually.)

Alice, our dear little Maine coon cat, was dying of cancer. There was nothing we could do, Dr. B said, but keep her comfortable.

Shakespeare, ever loyal, was at least eleven years old, an aging cur no matter what years you counted in, dog or human. He wasn't going to live forever; big dogs rarely lived past twelve to fifteen years.

Freddie was, well, still Freddie. It was safe to assume that sooner rather than later it would be just me and Freddie in this cottage on the lake. Five years, $400 worth of obedience training, and much practice later, Freddie and I were pals. No, he didn't ring the bell to go out or high-five me on command, but thanks to Karen and lots of practice he would sit and stay whenever I asked him. At least most of the time.

He was more gracious to our guests, male and female, and more courteous to other animals, canine and feline. In fact, it had been Freddie who first noticed that there was something wrong with Alice. He kept sniffing her legs, poking his nose into her long feathery tiger fur and whining. When she started to limp, I thought it was Freddie's fault, that he had hurt her somehow.

But Dr. B confirmed that Freddie had not injured the cordial little kitty; she was limping because cancer had spread throughout her body, and it was affecting her mobility. Dogs have been known to detect cancer by smell alone—and as a beagle Freddie had one heck of a good nose.

The day I had to put Alice down was a very bad day. Dr. B told me that when the time came, I would know it, and I did. I came home late one night after a short business trip to find that in my absence she'd disappeared into my bedroom, and curled up on a blanket in the corner to suffer in peace.

"She won't leave," Mikey said. "I didn't know what to do. So I put the litter box in there with her."

"That's fine, honey. We knew this was coming." Dr. B had prescribed meds to help keep her comfortable until it was time for her to go.

Freddie followed me through the living room to my bedroom door, and whimpered. He looked up at me, big brown eyes sadder than I had ever seen them. "I know, Freddie. I know."

Alice, always a little kitty, was thin as a feather now, and just as light. I gathered her up in my arms, and looked into her once beautiful green eyes, now vacant with pain. Freddie stood up on his back legs, and sniffed at her with a low bellow.

"It's okay, Freddie. Nothing more we can do for her now." It was late now, too late to call Dr. B. So I settled under the covers with Alice for the night. Freddie, who usually slept with Mikey on his bed in his room, insisted on sleeping with Shakespeare on the floor next to me and Alice that night. None of us got much sleep. I kept waking up to check on Alice, and the dogs kept silent sentinel as I caressed the poor ailing creature.

The next day I called Dr. B and he asked me to bring Alice in that afternoon. I dropped Shakespeare off at the groomer and then came back to the house. Mikey was at the mall with his buddies, so it was just me and Alice and Freddie. I sat cross-legged on the couch, cradling Alice loosely in my arms on my lap. Freddie planted his bullet body at my feet, his soft wet nose on my knee, tucked up against her weary little frame. We sat there together, unmoving, for hours.

Finally, it was time. I lifted Alice up, and untangled my legs. I drew my purse over my shoulder, careful not to disturb the limp kitty, whom I held as lightly as a football in the crook of my right arm. A sober Freddie trod lightly behind me. The usually lively beagle stood there somber, watchful and quiet and still, as I carried the tiny cat out of the house. I turned to shut the door behind me, and Freddie gazed up at me, as if he knew that he'd never see Alice again. Maybe he did.

At the animal hospital, Dr. B was at his most kind and compassionate.

"I didn't know if it was time or not," I said. "But she looks so . . . ." My voice trailed off as I choked back tears.

"You did fine," he said gently. "It's definitely time."

I nodded.

"We'll sedate her first," Dr. B said as he gave Alice a shot. "She'll go to sleep, and then we'll administer the dosage." I stroked Alice, whose eyes closed as she drifted to sleep, never to wake again. I didn't cry. I watched Dr. B as he slipped in the IV.

"It won't be long now. I'll leave you some private time," he said quietly, and left the room.

"Sweet kitty," I crooned to my dear little cat as she drew her last breaths.

And suddenly it was over. She was gone. Dr. B came back into the room, and shared his condolences. I thanked him and left. He would have Alice cremated, as burying her at home was not an option as we lived on the lake.

Dry-eyed, I left the animal hospital and drove home. I had never had to put an animal down before. Isis had died in my arms—and Alice did, too. The only difference was that I knew it was coming.

At home, Freddie was waiting for me. Shakespeare was still at the groomer; Mikey was still at the mall. I lit a fire in the fireplace, even though it wasn't cold. I poured myself a glass of red wine, and curled up on the couch with a quilt. Freddie trotted over to me, and placed his generous paws on my lap. I petted him absently, scratching his ears. I stared into the fire, and raised my glass.

"To Alice," I said to Freddie. Freddie cocked his head, and his ears fell to one side. I leaned over, and allowed him a rare lick on the face. Then I settled back against the pillows, my legs tucked under me, and began to cry. Freddie whimpered, and jumped up on the couch, circling into the curve of my thighs.

And for once I let him stay right there.

Freddie had known Alice was sick before I did. He'd tried to tell me about her illness, but I'd read him all wrong. It wasn't the first time I'd accused Freddie falsely of bad behavior. It probably wouldn't be the last. It was hard for me to change longtime impressions, even when they misled me. It was hard for Freddie to change his longtime behaviors, even when they misled him.

But as we'd learned the long, hard way: Practice *does* make perfect. Training *does* work—but only if you train yourself as well as your dog.

"Sorry, Freddie," I said as I buried my tear-stained face in his silky fur.

Freddie licked my tears away. Then he nudged his nose under my hand. As the fire roared, and we mourned Alice together on the couch, I realized that I may not need that horse after all.

When Mikey turned seventeen, my folks drove a 2002 Ford Escort Z2 across the country as a late birthday present for their favorite high-school senior. Dad bought all my kids cars when they were old enough to drive—and now it was Mikey's turn.

"Ill," Mikey said.

"That means he likes it," I translated for my parents.

"We know that," said my mother.

"Of course you do," I said. Mikey spent a week every summer with his grandparents in Vegas before going to see his father. On these visits his grandparents took him bowling, shopping, and to the movies. They watched a lot of TV and played video games—or at least watched Mikey play. Thanks to Mikey, they were fairly well versed in such pop-culture classics as *Pineapple Express*, skater/surf clothes, and *The Colbert Report*. "My apologies."

Dad and Mikey spent the next few days bonding over the many teachable joys of three-point turns, backing up, and parallel parking, while Mom and I prepared for the open house celebrating Mikey's new wheels.

The weather was perfect the day of the party—another beautiful autumn day on the lake. We sat down on the patio by the water, drinking wine and watching the water-skiers and fishermen and canoers and kayakers out on the glistening great pond. Friends and neighbors and teenagers came and went all afternoon. Shakespeare and Freddie flanked the Colonel, calm as the cool breeze that rippled the surface of the water.

"He's like a different dog," my mother said of Freddie. "So friendly, so well behaved, so *good*."

It was true. Freddie was on his best behavior; he actually boasted a best-behavior mode now. He'd come a long way, this rambunctious beagle, and this afternoon was proof of that. Freddie had not been invited to one of our parties since he was a puppy at that long-ago open house we'd hosted when we first moved into the cottage five years before. Ever since his tumultuous adolescence, we had to board the excitable beast at the kennel overnight whenever we entertained. This party was a first for the adult Freddie.

"I guess he's growing up." I looked across the patio at Mikey and his teenage friends, flipping more burgers on the Weber. They'd already eaten all the prepared party food, and now that all the adult guests had eaten all they could possibly eat, the teenagers were starting all over again with the remaining contents of my fridge. "They're *all* growing up."

"They're good kids," said my father, which was the highest praise he ever afforded young people.

"Yes, they are. And they love you." Mikey and his friends had spent virtually all of their spare time hanging out with my dad on the dock, fishing and grilling and talking sports. Boys always loved the Colonel.

"Where are their fathers?"

"Brian and Ross have parents who are still together, so they see their dads all the time. But Wilbur's parents are divorced," I said. "He lives with his single mom. Just like Mikey and me."

"*Hmpph,*" my father said.

"Let's face it, Dad, there isn't a boy on the planet who wouldn't benefit from time with you. You should start a camp. I'll sign Mikey up ASAP."

"Mikey turned out just fine," my mother said.

"Agreed," said my father.

I beamed. "Yes, he did."

"They all did," my mother said.

"I could never have done it without you," I said.

"Not true," the Colonel said.

"Don't you dare cry," my mother said.

"I won't," I said, and changed the subject. "Pretty soon it will just be me and the dogs."

"Shakespeare's getting old," Dad warned. "He must be at least twelve years old by now. That's getting up there for a big dog."

"Me and Freddie then," I said with a sigh. At the sound of his name, the pugnacious pooch trotted over to me, and placed his silky-eared head on my knee. I scratched his solid little neck, and he closed his big brown eyes, wriggling his bulletbody with pleasure.

"Isn't Freddie going to college with Mikey?" asked Dad.

"Great idea!" I said. "Thanks, Dad."

"I heard that, Mom," called Mikey from the picnic table, where he and the boys were chowing down the last of the burgers. "No way."

"Way," I answered.

"Sorry, no dogs at the dorm." Mikey grinned. "Those are the rules. Gotta follow the rules. Right, Papa Colonel?"

Dad grinned, too. "That's right."

"Just me and Freddie," I said. "Perfect."

"What about Joel?" asked my mother.

I laughed. "Mom, you never give up, do you?"

"I hope you invited him to the party," my mother said. "He's practically remodeled the entire house for you."

"Not the whole house, Mom. There's still the bathroom to redo, and I'd love to change the kitchen around," I said.

"Yes, I know," my mother said. "But did you invite him to the party?"

"He knows about the party," I said. "But you know as well as I do that he'll never come."

"He's just running late."

"The party's nearly over, Mom. Everyone's come and gone but us and the boys." I smiled. "He's not coming. And that's okay. Really." I let Freddie lick my face. "Besides, who needs a man when I've got Freddie?"

My mother raised an eyebrow. My dad grinned. Mikey laughed.

"See, Mom, I knew you'd love Freddie, sooner or later." Mikey walked over to the side of the patio where his grandparents and I sat with the dogs.

"Much later," I said.

Freddie started to howl, pulling away from me abruptly and dashing up the hill.

"Never say never." Mikey pointed up the hill to the cottage.

Around the corner, under the pergola he'd built with those ham-fisted hands, came Joel.

"I invited him myself," my mother said.

"Of course you did," I said.

"I knew he would come." My mother beamed. "He's a trainable man. *Not* intense."

"Golden Retriever," my father said.

"I'm not sure I need a dog," I said. "Or a husband."

My mother stared at me.

"I have my work, my house, my dogs." I took a deep breath. "My youngest child is leaving the nest, but I have a granddaughter now. And another on the way. My life is full."

"Yes, but—"

"Need a husband?" I asked my mother.

My mother smiled as she answered me. "Get a dog."

"And I've got Freddie."

Freddie ran to Joel, tail wagging. Shakespeare followed suit. Joel waved his hellos, and then sat down with us on the patio. The dogs settled down once again, this time at Joel's feet.

"Joel," my mother said, "what about that bathroom?"

The moral of my dog story is this: You *can* fix your life. All it takes is a dogged determination, a nose for trouble, and—when all else fails— the courage to howl at the moon.

Freddie taught me that.

Acknowledgments

So many two-legged and four-legged animals to thank! First, my love and gratitude to my parents and my children, who've had to live with the fact that I'm a writer—and have always done so with grace and generosity.

I'd like to acknowledge the men I have loved, and who have loved me: You know who you are.

Thank you also to the nicest next-door neighbor ever, Steve Stewart, and to the world's finest vet, Dr. Jeffrey M. Barrow, and everyone at the Marshfield Animal Hospital, especially Karen Lambrecht, dog trainer extraordinaire.

And a special shout-out to the friends who read early drafts of this book: Gina Panettieri, Trish MacGregor, Hallie Ephron, Hank Phillippi Ryan, Laura Daly, Sandy Ryan, Joel McMillan, Rich Krevolin, and Beth Gissinger, as well as my fellow and sister writers in the Mystery Writers of America, the Monday Murder Club, and of course my beloved Scribe Tribe.

Most importantly, perhaps, thank you to my publisher Karen Cooper, who believed in this project from the start, and my editor Meredith O'Hayre, who read the manuscript way too many times.

Thanks also to Susan Reynolds, Carol Mouledous Ammons, Renée Bravo Spratt, Casey Ebert, Frank Rivera, Denise Wallace, Sue Beale, Phil Sexton, Jon Ackerman, Leslie Hendrickson, Matt Glazer, Heather Padgen, and Wendy Simard.

About the Author

Photo by Susan Reynolds

Paula Munier has been a dog person her whole life. Raised by a father with a penchant for Weimaraners, vizslas, and Great Danes, on her tenth birthday she got her first dog of her own—a black miniature French poodle named Rogue. Since then she has shared her life with numerous dogs, cats, fish, and a bearded lizard, all of which together caused far less trouble than just one small beagle named Freddie. She lives on the South Shore of Massachusetts with her family and two dogs. Learn more at *www.fixingfreddie.com.*